Libellus de Historia

Latin History Reader
for use with

Latin for Children: Primer C

Acknowledgements

Classical Academic Press would like to thank **Gaylan Dubose** for his expertise and care in editing this text.

Libellus de Historia

Latin History Reader for use with
Latin for Children: Primer C

www.ClassicalAcademicPress.com

ISBN: 1-60051-016-7
EAN: 9781600510168

Book design & cover by:
Rob Baddorf

"Cui dono lepidum novum libellum . . ."
-Catullus

For my children, Michael, Matthew, and Katelyn, who
never tire of hearing the tales of George Washington,
Paul Revere, and other great Americans who have given
so much to preserve our beloved country.

Many thanks to my "other kids",
the 2005 - 2006 Latin Club at
Grace Academy of Georgetown,
who helped me improve upon
many of the stories within this
little book.

Latin For Children, Primer C
LATIN READER

Contents

Contents

Contents

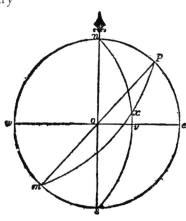

Contents

✲ N.B.

As this reader was designed to supplement *Latin for Children, Primer C*, the following grammar is assumed for all stories:

- 1st & 2nd conjugation, present system (i.e., present, imperfect, future tenses)
- 3rd conjugation verbs, present tense
- 1st, 2nd, & 3rd declension nouns and 3rd declension i-stem nouns
- 1st & 2nd declension adjectives
- irregular verbs *esse* & *īre*
- uses of the nominative case: subject, predicate
- uses of the genitive case: possession, partitive genitive
- uses of the accusative case: direct object, object of Latin prepositions
- use of the ablative case: object of Latin prepositions
- personal pronouns: *ego, tu, is, ea, id*
- cardinal and ordinal numerals, 1 – 10
- demonstrative adjective/pronouns: *hic, ille, iste*

Libellus dē Historiā, Pars C

A Little Book about History, Part C

Latin is a language unlike any other. One uses it not merely as a means to communicate with others regarding the happenings of the present, but also as a key to unlock the secret treasures of the past. It is therefore with greatest delight that we share with you this little book of 32 Latin stories that tell a few tales of treasures past. From the voyage of Columbus to the explorations of Lewis and Clark, from the Battle of Bunker Hill to the War of 1812, students will witness the birth pangs of America while applying the grammar tools of Latin that they have acquired.

Each story is keyed to the Latin grammar and vocabulary taught in Latin for Children, Primer C and the history taught through the Veritas Press Explorers to 1815 History Series. While the reader was originally conceived as a supplemental text to enhance the learning experience of the student using these curricula, it is not necessary to use either of them to benefit from and enjoy this reader. This little book has a user-friendly format in order to provide full support for even the most novice Latin teachers, regardless of the curriculum they choose.

Several helpful features are included to make this text easy to use by students, teachers, and parents. First, the book opens with a Table of Contents listing the grammar assumed for each story. This enables teachers to better select the appropriate material for their young translators. Next the reader will find a small glossary within each story. This glossary lists all new vocabulary words for that story not already taught in previous chapters of LFC's Primers A, B, and C, or seen in previous stories. Within each glossary the authors have also included their own notes that fully explain those grammatical constructions unfamiliar to students. On many occasions they have also included notes pertaining to the etymology of words or their historical significance. These should provide many opportunities to further class discussions about the readings. In addition, a comprehensive Glossary is included in the back, listing every word used throughout the reader. Each entry is accompanied by a reference to the chapter in which that word first appears. Lastly, readers will find a bibliography full of additional resources that may further integrate history lessons with Latin studies.

Finally, I would like to share with you my approach for both written and oral translations. This process is one I developed in my own classroom through the years; I find it to be very beneficial. Whether you choose this approach or develop one of your own, maintaining a consistent and systematic method of translating will make the experience more enjoyable for both students and teachers.

Step 1: Unfamiliar Vocabulary List

Students should make a list of all vocabulary they do not recognize or whose meaning they are uncertain of. While all vocabulary not glossed with a particular story is assumed to have already been learned or seen in previous chapters, students may have yet to seal these words in their minds. Putting this step before the actual translation may seem tedious at first. However, I guarantee that this discipline will make the translation process much smoother. Moreover, this exercise will reinforce the students' developing vocabulary and memorization skills. The more often a student must look up a given word, whose meaning eludes him, the better he will learn that word.

Step 2: Written Translation

I generally advise that students be divided into groups of two to three for this task. Particularly in the beginning, students who have little or no experience translating passages will find some security and confidence in working together. However, I find that groups larger than three have a more difficult time collaborating effectively to obtain a good translation. Other times, you may wish to have students work independently.

When I was a child daunted by an overwhelming task, my mother would often ask, "How do you eat an elephant? One bite at a time!" (The answer that I would not ever wish to eat an elephant was never accepted). Some students may at times feel overwhelmed by the length of a passage or even a sentence. Indeed it may appear to them to be of elephantine proportions. Encourage students to tackle their elephant one sentence at a time. When compound sentences appear complex, advise students to break the sentence into smaller pieces by looking for conjunctions, commas, parentheses, quotation marks, et cetera.

Now that the elephant has been carved up, here's some advice on how to chew the meaty morsels and not choke on them. Latin does have a general word order (S, O, V). Its sentence structure is more loose than English, but most prose does follow certain rules. Thus, each sentence may be approached with a Question and Answer Flow that should be familiar to students of Shurley Grammar. For the passages in this reader, this simple question pattern should suffice:

1. Where is the Verb (Linking or Action)? Parse: Tense, Person, Number.
2. Where is the Subject? Parse: Case, Number, Gender.
3. Any Adjectives modifying the Subject? Parse: Case, Number, Gender.
4. Do we need a Direct Object, Predicate, or Indirect Object? Why? Parse: Case, Number, Gender.
5. Any Adjectives modifying the D.O. /P.N. /I.O.? Parse: Case, Number, Gender.
6. Are there any Prepositions? What case does the Preposition take? Where is the Object of the Preposition? Parse: Case, Number, Gender.
7. Any Adjectives modifying the O.P.? Parse: Case, Number, Gender.
8. Any word(s) left? Parse: Case, Number, Gender or Tense, Person, Number. How does this word fit in our sentence? Why?

Repeat this process for each sentence and each subordinate clause within a sentence, and before long the elephant will be pleasantly digested!

Step 3: Oral Translation

Many classrooms may wish to end the translation process with a written exercise. While that is certainly a sufficient end for some, I feel they are missing out on a wonderful opportunity. Oral translation is my favorite part of Latin class both as a student and as a teacher. This is a wonderful exercise that has so many benefits. First, it builds great confidence in the students for they are truly reading a Latin story. Second, it works to develop oral language skills, which students will need in learning any modern language they may choose to study. Finally, oral practice helps in laying a foundation for the Rhetoric Stage, the capstone of the Trivium.

If possible, arrange students in a circle or other arrangement in that enables class members to participate and interact well with one another and the teacher. Allow them their Latin passage and unfamiliar vocabulary list, but do not allow them their English translations. We all know that they can read English; this exercise is to practice reading Latin.

Before you begin reading, it is important to give everyone, including the teacher, permission to make mistakes, no matter how big they seem. No one is fluent in Latin yet. We are all learning.

One by one have students read aloud; first in Latin then in English. Longer sentences may be divided up if needed. If a student appears to be stuck, choking on a large piece of elephant, guide them through the sentence using the questions listed above. Then, ask them to re-translate the sentence smoothly on their own. Occasionally ask a student to re-translate a sentence already translated by someone else, but in a slightly different way.

Step 4: Reading Comprehension

Teaching students how to read for comprehension and specific information is an important goal at the grammar stage. It need not be limited to English grammar classes. Each story in this reader is followed by a few reading comprehension questions. They may certainly be used as a written exercise. However, I recommend asking them orally following the time of oral translation. It gives students a thrill to know they are having a Latin conversation, while at the same time exercising both their oral and reading comprehension skills. This entire translation process, from vocabulary to oral discussion, should take three class periods with a little bit of homework; possibly four periods if you prefer all work to be done in class.

Sight Translation

After orally translating a few stories as recommended above, students may be ready to take their Latin reading comprehension to a new level, sight translation. Try reading a story aloud to students as they silently read along. You may wish to read it to them more than once. Then ask them a few simple questions using the interrogatives they are familiar with. Use the reading comprehension questions at the bottom to guide you. The class will be amazed at how much they are able to glean from a story without first fully translating. Then walk them through the process of an oral translation. Offer as much vocabulary help as possible. The goal of this exercise is to continue to train their minds to analyze language and its grammatical structure.

As you read through these stories, be sure to take the time not only to enjoy the vocabulary and grammar contained in this little book, but the stories used to demonstrate them as well. This book contains many narratives guaranteed to draw students into pivotal moments of American History. Translate an actual transcript from the Salem Witch Trials; read a farmer's story about his experience during the First Great Awakening; ride with Paul Revere through the American colonies. When you have reached the end of journey, you will find an appendix containing the Pledge of Allegiance and the Star-Spangled Banner in Latin. Truly, Libellus de Historia is a Latin reader that no American student should be without!

CAPUT I

Prīnceps Henricus, Nauta
MCCCXCIV - MCCCCDX A.D.

Henricus "Nauta" prīnceps Lūsitānōrum est. Annō

Henry ~~is the~~ "The Navigator" is the prince of the Portugese.

MCCCXCIV, in Lūsitāniā nascitur. Lūdum nauticōrum fundat.

In the year 1394, he is born in Portugal. He astablished a school of mariners.

Nāvigātiōnibus pecūniam dat. Haec facta Henricī viam ab Africā

He gives money to the voyage. This act of Henry opens up a

ad Asiam patefaciunt. Multī magistrī chartographiae, astrologiae,

road ~~from~~ africa to asia. Many teachers ~~who~~ who

et nauticōrum in hunc lūdum veniunt.

study ~~cartography~~ ~~maps~~ astronomy, and sailing come in this school.

Hī magistrī navarchīs Prīncipis Henricī doctrīnam ad

These teachers give ~~...~~ navy teaching the

nāvigātiōnēs aptam dant. Ūnus ex navarchīs Prīncipis Henricī

Suited for navigation. One out of the Captains of Prince Henry

prīmōs servōs ex Africā portat. Prīnceps Henricus plusquam

carries prime slaves out of Africa. Prince Henry sends out more than quinquāginta nāvigātiōnēs mittit. Sed Prīnceps Henricus nōn nauta

50 navigators. But Prince Henry is not a

vērus est et numquam cum nāvigātiōnibus nāvigat.

true sailors, and never sailed with the navigators

    Nulla nāvigātiōnum Prīncipis Henricī Asiam accedit. Ūnus

NONE of the navigators of Prince Henry reaches Asia.

ex navarchīs Serram Leōnum accedit.

One out of the Ship Captains reaches the range of lions!

Prīnceps Henricus, Nauta

GLOSSARY & NOTES:

Henricus, ī, m., Henry

Lūsitanī, ōrum, m. pl., the Portuguese.

annō, = in the year...

> ablative of time within which. This construction using the ablative without a preposition is used to demonstrate the time within which an event occurs
> [*See AG 423*].

nascitur = he is born < nascor, nascī, natus sum, to be born.

> This is a deponent verb. Deponent verbs are passive in form, but active in meaning.

nauticus, a, um, adj., nautical, naval. (neuter pl. as noun, translate "nautical things.")

fundō, āre, āvī, ātum, to lay the foundation, to found, establish

nāvāgatio, ōnis, f., a sailing, voyage.

dēnique, adv., at last, finally

factum, ī, n., deed, act

patefaciō, patefacere, patefēcī, patefactum, to make open, make clear. *Patefaciunt, they open up...*

chartographia, ae, f., cartography, study of map-making

> The word is not classical. To express what we mean by "map" the Romans would have used the phrase, *tabula geographica*.

astrologia, ae, f., the study of the stars.

> *Astrum* + *logia*, the study of the stars. The term *astrologia* was the original term which covered the science we know as *astronomy*. In the Renaissance, scientists began to make a distinction between the study of the stars for divination (astrology) and the study of the stars for purely empirical reasons (astronomy).

navarchus, ī, m., ship's captain

doctrīnam, The abstract noun *doctrīna* comes from the verb *doceō, ēre*, to teach. *doctrīna* thus refers to a body of information which is imparted by teaching.

ūnus ex navarchīs, When one wants to express "one of ...", one uses the preposition **"ē/ex"** + the ablative. cf. *ē pluribus ūnum* (one out of many) [*See AG 346.2*].

plusquam, adv., more than

quinquāginta, indeclinable numerical adj., fifty

mittō, mittere, mīsī, missum, to send, dispatch

numquam, adv., never

nullus, a, um, adj. no one, none. One expresses "none of..." with nūllus and a noun in the genitive case (called the "partitive genitive")

accedō, accedere, accessī, accessum, to reach, get to, approach.

Serra Leōnum, lit., "moutain range of lions," modern day Sierra Leon, a country in West Africa.

> The original Portuguese name of this West African region was "Serra Leonem," meaning "mountain range of lions." The words sierra (Spanish) and serra (Portuguese) come from the Latin serra, ae, f., saw. The word was applied to particularly jagged mountain ranges which appeared saw-like in profile. N.B. that we get the words serrate and serrated from this Latin root.

RESPONDĒ LATĪNĒ:

1. Quī in hunc lūdum veniunt?

2. Quem magistrī docent?

3. Estne Prīnceps Henricus nauta vērus? Cūr?

Quī (pl.) – who?
Quem – whom?
Estne – is he?
Cūr – why?
Minime – no
ita vero - yes

CAPUT II

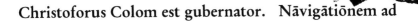

Christoforus Colom
MCDXCII A.D.

Christoforus Colom est gubernator. Nāvigātiōnem ad

lūdum Prīncipis Henricī discēbat. Christoforus terram esse orbem

putat. Isabellae, Rēgīnae Hispāniae nūntiat, "Id probābō, terram

esse orbem dēmōnstrābō, ad Indiam nāvigābō!" Christoforus

rēgīnam mandāre eō pecūniam et nāvēs rogat. Sed rēgīna eās

nōn mandābit. Iterum et iterum rēgēs, Rēgem Ferdinandum et

Rēgīnam Isabellam, rogat. Sed semper respondunt "minime!," quod

Christoforus magnum praemium rogat. Tandem, Ludovicus dē

Christoforus Colom

Santangel, aerārī praefectus rēgis, rēgem prō Christoforō suadit.

Rēgēs pecūniam et trēs navēs mandant.

Annō Dominī MCCCCXCII, Christoforus Colom nāvigat.

Nāvēs duōs mensēs nāvigant. Duodecimō diē Octōbris, nauta

terram videt. Christoforus hanc terram esse Indiam putat.

Ad Hispāniam redit et multa nova mīraque refert. Rēgēs eō

appellātiōnem, Ōceanicis Classis Praefectum, dant. Pontifex

Alexander VI, Hispānus, lineam confiniī indicat et ōceanum inter

Hispāniam et Lusitaniam dīvidit.

Christoforus Colom

GLOSSARY & NOTES:

Christoforus Colom, m., Christopher Columbus

> This was the manner in which Christopher Columbus's own signature was translated when his letters were published in Latin. In his own lifetime, he was referred to as Colom, instead of Columbus. Today, his descendants bear the surname Colon.

gubernātor, gubernātōris, m., navigator

nāvigātiō, nāvigātiōnis, m., navigation

ad, best translated here as 'at'

terram esse orbem = the earth is a globe

> Indirect Discourse. Literally, " He thinks the earth to be a globe." The phrase may also be translated more loosely, "the earth is a globe. " [AG, 577, 581]

Hispānia, ae, f., Spain

iterum, adv., again

sed, conj., but

semper, adv., always

minime = no!

magnum praemium – As a reward for his promised discovery, Columbus asked for a percentage of all riches harvested, the title and powers of Viceroy of all lands discovered, and the grand title Admiral of the Ocean Fleet.

quod, conj., because

tandem, adv., finally

Ludovicus dē Santangel, m., Luis de Santangel

> Luis de Santangel, treasurer to the King and a great help to Columbus, convinced the King that the benefits of such a discovery would be worth Columbus' price.

aerārī praefectus = treasurer

annō, ablative of time when = in the year

> The ablative case is used to denote the time when an event occurs. The English prepositions "in" or "on" may be used when translating

this construction.

[AG, 423]

duōs mensēs, accusative of duration of time = for two months

> The accusative case is used to show the extent of time over which an event occurs. The English prepositions "to" or "for" may be used when translating this construction.

duodecimō diē, ablative of time when = on the twelfth day

Octōber, Octōbris, m., October

terram esse Indiam = the land is India (literally, the land to be India)

> Indirect discourse (see above)

refert = he brings back < irregular verb, *referō, referre,* to bring back

multa nova mīraque, neuter plural

> Substantive adjectives. Adjectives placed in the neuter plural without an accompanying noun may be translated as "things": many new and wonderful things [AG, 288]

appellātio, appellātiōnis, f., title

Ōceanicis Classis Praefectum = Admiral of the Ocean Fleet

Hispānus, a, um, adj. Spaniard

lineam confiniī = line of demarcation

> The line of demarcation declared by Pope Alexander VI, May 4, 1493, ran from the Arctic Pole down to the Antarctic Pole 100 leagues West of the Cape Verde and Azores Islands. Anything to the East was declared to belong to Portugal, the West was given to Spain. This ruling, or bull, issued by the Pope, himself a Spaniard, favored Spain.

Christoforus Colom

RESPONDĒ LATĪNĒ:

1. Ubī Christoforus nāvigātiōnem discit?

2. Quī sunt rēgēs Hispāniae?

3. Quam appellātiōnem rēx Christoforō dat?

Ubī – where?
Quī (pl.) – who?
Quam – what?

CAPUT III

Magellanus Orbem Circumnāvigat
MDXIX – MDXXII A.D.

Ferdinandus Magellanus navarchus Lūsitānus est. Prīmus

orbem circumnāvigat. Classem quinque nāvium iubet. Rēx

Hispānōrum, Carolus I, nāvigātiōnī nōbilī pecūniam dat. Nāvēs

classis sunt, in linguā Lūsitānā, Conception, San Antonio, Saniago,

Trinidad, et Victoria. In viā, quīdam ex nautīs sēditiōnem faciunt.

Aliī nautae dūcem sēditiōnis necant et duōs ex comitibus eius

relinquunt.

Magellanus Orbem Circumnāvigat

Magellanus viam ad Mare Pācificum invenit. Hodiē,

hanc viam "Fretum Magellanī" appellāmus. Ante Magellanus

nāvigātiōnem perficit, dux Lapu Lapu et comitēs eum in Insulīs

Philippinīs necant. Annō MDXXII, ūna nāvis, Victoria, cum XVIII

superstitibus nautīs, ad Hispāniam redit.

Magellanus Orbem Circumnāvigat

GLOSSARY AND NOTES

Ferdinadus Magellanus, Ferdinand Magellan

prīmus, a, um, adj., the first.

> To say "he was the first to..." in Latin, one simply uses the adjective prīmus to modify the subject.

orbem, The regular Latin expression for the "known world" was *orbis terrārum,* but we are specifically concerned with the world with respect to its geographically spherical nature. The ancients thought of the world as a disc, and this is what orbis originally means: a ring, a circuit, any two-dimensional circle, see L&S entry.

circumnāvigō, āre, āvī, ātum, (circum + nāvigō): use your knowledge of Latin to figure out what this word means!

pecūniam, < **pecus, udis,** n., cattle. In early Rome, before the introduction of coinage, one's wealth was reckoned by the number of cattle and other livestock one owned. This was the case in the Old Testament, as well as in many other societies, ancient and modern.

classis, is, f., fleet (of ships)

Hispānī, ōrum, m.pl., the Spanish

Carolus, ī, m., Charles (cf. Carolus magnus = Charlemagne; Carolina, "land of Charles")

pecūniam dō, to pay for, fund

quīdam, quaedam, quiddam, a certain one, certain ones.

> Quīdam takes the prepositional phrase "*ē*/ex" + the ablative.

sēditio, ōnis, f., mutiny, armed uprising. **Sēditiōnem facere,** to mutiny

faciō, ere, fēcī, factum, to make, do; **faciunt,** they make

alius, a, ud, adj., another, other

relinquō, ere, relīquī, relictum, depart from, leave, forsake, abandon.

pācificus, a, um, adj., peaceable, peaceful

inveniō, invenīre, invēnī, inventum, to discover the existence of, find

fretum, ī, n., strait, sound

Philippinus, a, um, adj., of Philip, Philippine

Magellanus Orbem Circumnāvigat

The Philippines were so-called after King Philip II of Spain, who organized the first colony in 1565. Lapu Lapu was the name of the chief who fought and killed Magellan.

perficiō, perficere, perfēcī, perfactum, to complete, finish; **perficit,** he/she/it completes

Our word "perfect" comes from this Latin root. "Perfect" means "finished."

superstes, itis, adj., or noun, survivor.

RESPONDĒ LATĪNĒ:

1. Quis est Magellanus?

2. Quid Magellanus facit?

3. Quis eō pecūniam dat?

4. Ubī est Fretum Magellanī?

CAPUT IV

Victōria Hispāna
Saeculum MDC A.D.

Saeculō post prīmam Christoforī Colom nāvgātiōnem, Hispānia

et mediam et merīdiānam Americam vincit. Sīc, hoc saeculum

"Victoriam Hispānam" appellāmus.

Ūnus ex explorātōribus Hispanīs, Ferdinand Cortesius,

magnum imperium Aztecōrum ferōcum vincit. Prīmum, Cortesius

et comitēs rēgem Aztecōrum, Montezumam, necant. Deinde,

exercitum ingentem et cīvitātem veterem Aztecōrum perdunt.

Dēnique, Cortesius et comitēs Honduriam et paeninsulam

Californiae explōrant.

Annō MDXIII, alius explōrātōrum Hispanōrum, Ponce

de Leon, ad terram Flōridam nāvigat. Fontem adulēscentiae

perpetuae quaerit. Quamquam nōn hanc fontem fabulōsam, tamen

paeninsulam amoenam et fēcundam invenit. Hodiē, multī ad

Flōridam migrant et ibi habitant. Etiamnunc, cēterī illum fontem

quaerunt.

Victōria Hispāna

GLOSSARY & NOTES

saeculum, ī, n., generation; more generally, a span of one hundred years, a century.

> **saeculō**, ablative of time when = in the century

medius, a, um, adj., the middle. It modifies the noun, and is translated "middle of...".

et...et, both...and

sīc, so, thus, in this way

> The way Spanish speakers say "yes" (si) comes from the Latin *sīc*.

explōrātor, ōris, m., explorer

> This word, in classical prose, meant a scout or spy, in the military sense. The same is true of the cognate verb, *explōrō*. We may use these words because the meaning stretched over time to include what we mean by "explorer/explore."

Ferdinandus Cortesius, Hernando Cortez.

> *Ferdinandus* is the usual Latin form of Hernando. Surnames, during this period, were frequently not Latinized, but Cortez's was rendered into this language.

Aztecus, ī, m./**a, ae**, f., a native inhabitant of Mexico

> The word "Aztec" was not applied to this people group as a whole until the 19th century. The natives called themselves "Mexica," hence the name of the modern country.

ferox, ferōcis, adj., fierce, wild, warlike

prīmum, *adv.*, first, (not used as an adjective here. It introduces a series of events. The other events in the series are marked by *deinde*, next, and *dēnique*, finally.)

Montezuma, ae, m., Montezuma

> We will treat this name as a first declension masculine noun, like *agricola* or *nauta*.

ingens, ingentis, adj., huge

exercitum, acc., sg., m., army < **exercitus, ūs**, m., trained army.

> This is a fourth declension noun. See Primer C chapter 21 for a chart.

vetus, eris, adj., old, ancient

perdō, perdere, perdidī, perditum, to destroy, ruin, do away with.

Honduria, ae, f., Honduras

paeninsula, ae, f., peninsula

> *Paene.* (almost, all but) + *insula*, originally, two words. Thus a peninsula is an "almost-island."

California, ae, f., California.

> The modern area known as Baja, California, is actually in Mexico. Check it out on a *tabula geographica*!

Ponce dē Leon, same in English and Latin

> In de Leon's text *Sancti Ephiphanii ad Physiologum*, a Latin translation and commentary on Greek saint's sermons, de Leon, a very learned man, chose not to Latinize his name. This trend continues to this day, as most modern names are no longer Latinized in Latin texts. We will Latinize most Christian names in the following stories, but surnames will not be Latinized unless there is an evidence that the name has been correctly and authentically Latinized in the past.

Flōridus, a, um, adj., flowering, blooming, beautiful

fons, fontis, m., spring, fountain, well-source

perpetuus, a, um, adj., continuous, uninterupted

adulēscentia, ae, f., youth. cf. adulēscēns, entis, c., a young man or woman

quaero, ere, sivi, sītum, to look for, strive after, seek

quamquam...tamen, although...nevertheless

fābulōsus, a, um, adj., fabled, famous in stories. (compare to *fabula*)

amoenus, a, um, adj., pleasant, lovely, esp. of places.

fēcundus, a, um, adj., fertile, good for growing crops.

migrō, āre, āvī, ātum, to move, immigrate

etiamnunc = etiam + nunc, even now

Victōria Hispāna

RESPONDĒ LATĪNĒ:

1. Quem Cortesius vincit?

2. Quis est Rēx Aztecōrum?

3. Ubī est Fons Adulēscentiae?

4. Quis illum fontem quaerēbat?

CAPUT V

Samuhel dē Champlain

MDLXX – MDCXXXV A.D.

Samuhel dē Champlain in familiam nāvalem nātus est. Et pater et

patruus erant magistrī nāvium. Ubī Samuhel erat adulēscēns, ad

multōs distantēs locōs cum eīs nāvigābat.

Nunc Samuhel, vir, terrās Novae Galliae explōrat. Audāx

explōrātor sursum deorsum lītus nāvigat, multās chartographiās

facit, et bonus amīcus Indigenōrum fit. Samuhel Indigenās et

morēs eōrum honōrat. Mercātūram cum gente Indigenā, nomine

Huron, constituit. Huron gēns eum oppugnāre hostēs, nomine

Samuhel dē Champlain

Iroquois, rogat. Samuhel exercitum Indigenum secundum Sanctum

Laurentiam Flūmen ducit, et ingentem lacum invenit. Hunc lacum

"Champlain" appellat. Ibi est ferōx pugna. Samuhel trēs ducēs

necat, et Iroquois fugiunt. Haec victoria erit infēlix Gallīs; nam

Iroquois erunt ferōcēs hostēs eōrum multōs annōs.

Samuhel dē Champlain

GLOSSARY & NOTES:

<u>Samuhel de Champlain</u>, Samuel de Champlain, French Explorer

<u>nāvalis</u>, adj., naval

<u>nātus est</u> = was born < nascor, nasci, natus sum, deponent verb - to be born. Deponent verbs are passive in form, but active in meaning.

<u>patruus, ī, m.</u>, uncle (paternal uncle)

<u>magister, ī, m.</u>, captain (of a merchant ship)

<u>distans, distantis</u>, adj., distant

> In his youth Champlain sailed as far away as Central America and the West Indies. During this time he learned both navigation and chartography (the skill of map-making).

<u>sursum deorsum</u> = up and down

> Champlain sailed as far south as Cape Cod during his explorations of the North American Coast.

<u>fīō, fierī, factus sum</u>, irreg. verb, to become

<u>mōs, mōris, m.</u>, custom

<u>honōrō, āre, āvī, ātum</u>, to honor, respect

<u>mercātūra, ae, f.</u>, trade

> Champlain established a great system of trade with several native tribes. He traded them metal wares for their furs. Beaver pelts were the current fashion trend, and were in great demand throughout Europe. One tribe, the Huron, wanted more than just pots for their skins. They wanted Champlain's help in defeating their fierce enemy, the five Iroquois nations.

<u>Indigenus, a, um</u>, adj., native

<u>nomine</u> = by the name, called < nomen, nominis, n., name

<u>Iroquois</u>, Champlain sealed his friendship and trade business with the Huron tribe by helping them in their battles against the Iroquois. Unfortunately, the Iroquois greatly resented the Frenchman's alliance with the Huron, and caused the French settlers much grief for more than a hundred years after Champlain's death.

Samuhel dē Champlain

cōnstituō, cōnstituere, cōnstituī, cōnstitūtum, set up, establish.

What English word does this remind you of?

exercitum, acc., m., sing., army < exercitus, ūs, m. army

Laurentia, ae, m., Lawrence

lacum, acc., m., sing., lake < lacus, ūs, m. lake

fugiō, fugere, fūgī, fugitum, to flee

multōs annōs, accusative of duration of time = for many years

RESPONDĒ LATĪNĒ:

1. Ubī Samuhel explōrat?

2. Quid facit?

3. Quī gens est socius?

4. Quid erat officium et patrī et patruī?

Ubī – where?   Quid – what?   Quī – which?

CAPUT VI

Absēns Colōnia
MDLXXXV A.D.

Iohannes Albus ad Virginiam nāvigābat. Virginia est colōnia in

Americā. Ibi fīlia et neptis eius habitant. Ingens nāvis multās copiās

ad eās et colōnōs portābit. Iter trāns mare est longum et difficile,

sed Iohannes vidēre familiam studet. Tandem, nāvis ad novam

terram advenit. "Eheu!" Iohannes clāmat, "Ubī est colōnīa? Ubī est

mea familia?" Tōta colōnia est absēns, nullī colōnī sunt praesentēs.

Iohannes et sociī ubīque petunt, sed eōs nōn inveniunt. Ubī sunt eī?

Absēns Colōnia

Nēmō scit! Gravī cum corde Iohannes ad Britanniam redit.

Absēns Colōnia

GLOSSARY & NOTES:

colōnia, ae, f., colony

> This word referred to a settlement or colony of citizens sent from Rome, or the people inhabiting it.

Iohannes Albus, John White

> This name is taken from the Latin adjective meaning "white." Compare to the English derivative, "albino."

neptis, neptis, f.i., granddaughter

> The granddaughter referred to is Virginia Dare, the first child born of English parents in America. Her mother, Eleanor, was the daughter of the colony's Governor, John White.

studiō, studēre, studuī, to be eager

> You may have learned this verb as meaning, "to study". The translation best used here is "to be eager", another very common meaning of this verb.

adveniō, advenīre, advēnī, adventum, to arrive

eheu, interjection, alas!

meus, mea, meum, adj., my

ubīque, adv., everywhere

petō, petere, petīvī, petitum, to look for, go in search of

ubī, interrogative adv., where

nēmō, nēminis, m/f., nobody, no one

sciō, scīre, scivī , scītum, to know

cor, cordis, n. heart

RESPONDĒ LATĪNĒ:

1. Quō Iohannes Albus nāvigat?

2. Quid nāvis portat?

3. Ubī sunt colōnī ?

Quō – to where?   Quid – what?   Ubī – where?

CAPUT VII

Infēlix Colōnia
MDCVII A.D.

Annō Dominī MDCVII, trēs nāvēs centum quattuor virōs

et puerōs, nullās fēminās, ad Americam portābant. Multī facilēs

dīvitiās quaerēbant. Oppidum iuxtā flūmen, nomine Iacobum,

condēbant, cum incommodum in colōniam eōrum incidit. Iam est

annus MDCIX, tempus famis. Modo quadrāgintā virī vīvunt. Ignis

cōpiās eōrum perdidit. Ferōcēs Indigenae eōs oppugnant. Multī

virī sunt infirmī et aegrī. Relinquere oppidum volunt. Mox autem

fortūna mūtābit.

Infēlix Colōnia

Insequentī annō praefectus novus, Dominus De La Warr,

trecentōs virōs et auxilium ad oppidum feret. Annō MDCXII

Iohannes Rolfe, agricola, "viride aurum" creābit. Europaeī hanc

herbam amant, et agricolīs multam pecūniam dābunt. Iohannes

etiam Pocahantes, fīliam Rēgis Indigenae, in mātrimōnium dūcet.

Hoc mātrimōnium brevem pacem inter Indigenās et colōnōs creābit.

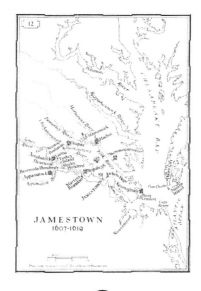

JAMESTOWN
1607-1619

Infēlix Colōnia

GLOSSARY & NOTES:

annō, ablative of time when

nullās fēminās = no women at all or not any women.

> Women were discouraged from these early voyages to America as colonists. The task of establishing a colony in primitive America was believed to be too harsh for women.

dīvitiae, ārum, f. pl., riches

Iacobus, ī, m., James

> The nearby river was named James for King James of England. The town was subsequently named Jamestown, being near this same river.

incommodum, ī, n., misfortune

iam, adv., now

famēs, famis, f., starvation

> tempus famis, This time period in the colony's history is often referred to as the "Starving Time."

incidō, incidere, incidī, incāsum, to occur (with in + acc., fall upon)

modo, adv., only

quadrāgintā, cardinal number, forty

perdidit = (perfect tense) it destroyed < *perdō, perdere, perdidī, perditum*, to destroy, ruin

Indigenae, This word may either be used as an adjective (native born) or as a noun of the first declension (native people). The word 'indigenous' is an English derivative.

aeger, aegra, aegrum, adj., sick

volunt = they wish < irreg., *volō, velle, voluī* – to wish

mox, adv., soon

insequens, insequentis, adj., following, next

Dominus De La Warr, nom., sing. m., Lord De La Warr

> Upon learning of the disasters which befell the Jamestown

colony, the Crown revoked the charter of the Virginia Company and appointed Lord De La Warr as the colony's new governor. The state of Delaware is named for him.

<u>feret</u> = he will bring < irreg. *fero, ferre, tulī, latum,* to bring, carry

<u>viride</u>, adj. modifying aurum, green

> The term 'green gold' (**viride aurum**) refers to the cash crop tobacco.

<u>in mātrimōnium dūcet</u> (idiom) = he will marry ____

> It was customary in ancient Rome to refer to a man as "leading his wife into marriage."

<u>brevem pacem</u>, The peace was to last for only ten years. In 1622 the local tribes attacked and destroyed the colony.

RESPONDĒ LATĪNĒ:

1. Quōmodo est colōnia infēlix?

2. Quid mūtat fortūnam eōrum?

3. Quid Iohannes Rolfe creat?

Quōmodo – how?   Quid – what?

CAPUT VIII

Nōbilis Nāvis
MDCXX A.D.

Mayflower onera pellium ē Britanniā ad Galliam et

Hispāniam saepe portābat. Deinde ad Britanniam vīnum referēbat.

Sed Augustō, annō dominī MDCXX, *Mayflower* et alia nāvis,

nomine *Speedwell*, ad Americam nāvigāvērunt. Onera pellium nōn

portāvērunt. Nunc multōs fortēs colōnōs portāvērunt. Nāvēs bis

revertērunt quod *Speedwell* rīmās egit. Vīgintī vectōrēs, infēlīcēs

et dēfessī, manēre optāvērunt. Dēnique, sextō diē Septembris, sōla

Mayflower cum centum duōbus vectōribus nāvigāvit.

Nōbilis Nāvis

Nāvigātiō erat difficilis et nōn celeris. In duōbus mensibus,

magna nāvis MMDCCL milia pasuum nāvigāvit (id est duo milia

passuum per hōram). Dēnique, nōnō diē Novembris, Americam

vīdērunt. In hāc novā terrā colōnī oppidum condidērunt. Hoc

oppidum "Novam Plymutam" appellāvērunt. *Mayflower* cum

colōnīs ūnum annum mānsit. In eā habitāvērunt dum casās

aedificāvērunt. Deinde, nōbilis nāvis ad patriam revertit.

Nōbilis Nāvis

GLOSSARY & NOTES:

nōbilis, nōbile, adj., famous, notable, noble

onus, oneris, n., load; cargo

> The Mayflower had been used as a cargo ship since 1609 when it was chartered by the Pilgrims. Upon its return to England, it returned to its former cargo routes.

pellis, pellis, f., hide, skin, fur

Britannia, ae, f., Britain.

> Another ancient word Britain or England is *Albion*. This Latin form for England was adopted by medieval writers from the writings of Ptolemy and Pliny. The name is thought to be of Celtic origin. However, the Romans are believed to have connected the ancient name with their own word *albus* (white), referring perhaps to the White Cliffs of Dover. *Albion* was used by many poets of the 18th century in reference to England.

Augustō, annō dominī, ablative of time when, the ablative case is used to express a specific date or time when an event occurs.

bis, adv., twice

revertō, revertere, revertī, revertus sum (compound of *vertere*), to turn back, return

rīmās egit, classical idiom = it cracked

> Twice in August the pilgrims sailed with both the Mayflower and Speedwell together. Each time the Speedwell began to leak (the second time they were already nearly 300 miles out into the Atlantic). The pilgrims determined the Speedwell not seaworthy and left her behind for the third and final attempt. Three launchings proved to be too much for twenty passengers, who decided to remain behind.

vīgintī, indeclinable numerical adj., twenty

vector, vectōris, m., passengers (on a ship)

sextō diē, ablative of time when (see above)

in duōbus mensibus, ablative of time within which – the ablative of time, sometimes preceded by the preposition *in* for emphasis, is used to express the amount of time within which something is accomplished.

Nōbilis Nāvis

milia passuum, mile (literally: a thousand of paces)

> This phrase is a partitive genitive literally meaning "a thousand of paces." *Pasuum* is the genitive plural of the 4th declension noun *passus, -ūs*. The fourth declension will be introduced in chapter 20. Miles were initially measured as one thousand paces. Thus, our English word 'mile' comes from the Latin word for thousand.

hōra, ae, f., hour

nōnō diē, ablative of time when (see above)

Novam Plymutam, f., Plymouth

> **Plymuta** is the name of the English town in civic records, with the qualifier *nova*, indicting that it belongs on this side of the pond. The name is seen here as a Cognitive Accusative. The accusative case is used when identifying the name by which something or someone is called.

ūnum annum, accusative of duration of time = **for one year.** The accusative case is used to express the duration of time something may require. The pilgrims continued to live on the Mayflower for one year after their arrival while they built the Plymouth colony.

dum, adv., while

Nōbilis Nāvis

RESPONDĒ LATĪNĒ:

1. Quāle onus Mayflower portābat?

2. Quid est nomen secundae nāvis?

3. Quot milia passuum nāvis nāvigāvit?

4. Ubī colōnī oppidum condidērunt?

Quāle – what kind of?
Quid – what?
Quot – how many?
Ubī – where?

CAPUT IX

Colōnia Nova Plymuta
Cīrca annum MDCXX A.D.

Colōnia Nova Plymuta in lītore Massachusettēnse erat. Cum

colōnī advēnērunt, multīs bonīs eguērunt. Sed Deum amāvērunt et

cūrae eius crēdidērunt. Quamquam dīligenter labōrāverant, erant

multās mortēs propter morbum et terrae inscientiam. In perīculīs

et temporibus acerbīs, Indigena, Tisquantum, colōniam adiūvāvit.

Tisquantum dē frūmentōrum cultūrā colōnōs docuit.

Colōnī dīligenter labōrāvērunt, frūmenta sēvērunt, et

autumnō messem cēpērunt. Cum Indigenīs et bene et libenter

Colōnia Nova Plymuta

cēnāvērunt. In convīviō, Deō prō cūrā eius grātiās maximās

ēgērunt. Sīc diem grātiārum constituērunt. Hodiē, Americānī

hunc diem conservāvimus, et hōs colōnōs "auctōrēs patriae nostrae"

appellāmus.

Colōnia Nova Plymuta

GLOSSARY & NOTES:

Massachusettēnsis, e, adj., of Massachusettes

Adding the ending **-ēnsis** to a place name is the common and classical way of creating its adjectival form.

cum, adv., when

This is not the preposition cum, but the temporal adverb cum.

bona, neut., acc., plur., < **bonus, a, um.** Here, the adjective is used as a noun, meaning literally "goods." Just as in English, one's "goods" are one's material possessions.

egeō, ēre, uī, (+ ablative) to want, to be in need of.

crēdō, crēdere, crēdidī, crēditum, (+ dative) to trust, trust in.

diligenter, adv., carefully, attentively

morbus, ī, m., sickness, illness

inscientia, ae, f., lack of knowledge, ignorance.

pereo, perīre, periī, peritum, to pass away, perish; *periērunt*, they perished

acerbus, a, um, adj., harsh, bitter, painful

Tisquantum, m., Squanto

frūmentum, The crop which Tisquantum taught the settlers to plant, American maize, was unknown in Europe, and thus no word existed in Latin to describe it. The word *frūmentum* is the closest approximation to the meaning, that is, a staple crop used to feed the populace.

cultūra, ae, f., culture, cultivation

diligenter, adv., (see above, diligens), carefully, attentively

serō, serere, sēvī, satum, to sow, plant

autumnus, ī, m., autumn. The noun is in the ablative. Like **annō,** which you have seen before, the case of this noun indicates the time within which something occurs. The fancy name for this is, you guessed it, the *ablative of time when*.

messis, is, f., harvest

capiō, capere, cēpī, captum, to seize, take; (here) take in

bene, adv., well

46

Colōnia Nova Plymuta

libenter, adv., willingly, gladly

convivium, iī, n., feast, banquet

> in conviviō, ablative of place where

agō, agere, ēgī, actum, to lead, carry out. With *gratiās* and a dative (of the person thanked). This is the Latin way of saying "give thanks."

> "Thank you" is *tibi agō grātiās*, and, also from this chapter, "you're welcome," is *lībenter*. But to be ready for polite society, one must know how to say please. A Roman of good upbringing would ask for the garum sauce, *amābō te*.

maximus, a, um, adj., greatest

> This is the superlative of *magnus*.

diem, masc., sg., acc., day < dies, ēī, m.

nostrae, our. This is a personal pronoun adjective. Like all Latin adjectives, it takes on the case, number, and gender of the noun modified. It does not reference the gender or number of the "we" in question.

Colōnia Nova Plymuta

RESPONDĒ LATĪNĒ:

1. Ubī erat Nova Plymuta?

2. Quis colōniam adiūvāvit?

3. Quid in convīviō fēcērunt?

Ubī – where?   Quis who?   Quid – what?

CAPUT X

Colōniae Novae Angliae

MDCXXX A.D.

Annō MDCXXX colōnī colōniam in Novā Angliā

condidērunt. Hōs colōnōs "puritanōs" appellāmus, quod Ecclēsiam

Anglicam purgāre voluērunt. Annō MDCXXVIII, Thoma Endicot

colōniam Puritanōrum in Novam Anglicam dēdūxit. Colōniam

"Salem" appellāvērunt. Duōs post annōs, Iohannes Winthrop,

gubernātor, mille Puritanī in Bostoniam dēdūxit. Cīvitātem prō

exemplō omnibus gentibus condere voluit.

Iohannes Cotton et aliī legēs et scholās in Bostoniā

condidērunt. Legēs et iūra ad praecepta Scriptūrārum constituere

voluērunt. Annō MDCXXXVI Ioannes Cotton Scholam Latīnam

Bostoniēnsem condidit. Etiamnunc discipulī litterās Latīnās et

Graecās ibi discunt.

Colōniae Novae Angliae

GLOSSARY & NOTES:

Anglia, ae, f., England. Anglicus, a, um, adj., English

> This word specifically refers to England, as opposed to Great Britain (**Britannia**), which includes Scotland, Wales, and the colonies.

Puritanus, Puritana, adj., "Puritan"

ecclēsia, ae, f., church

voluērunt, perfect tense, 3rd, pl. = they wanted < volō, velle, voluī, to wish, want. This verb takes an infinitive "wish to ___."

purgō, āre, āvī, ātum, to purify, cleanse

Thoma, ae, m., Thomas

dēdūcō, dēdūcere, dēdūxī, dēductum, to lead out. *Colōniam dēdūcere,* **to lead a colony.**

> This is one of the regular Latin idioms for leading a colony. Compare the compound verb *dē-dūcō* with both *dux* and *dūcō*.

Salem, the town of Salem, in Massachusetts

> The name Salem is from the Hebrew word *Shalom*, meaning "peace". Hebrew words, in the Vulgate and elsewhere, were typically not Latinized.

omnibus gentibus, dative case. The dative has the built in prepositions "to/for," and can be used as more than just an indirect object.

voluit, perfect, 3rd, sing. = he/she/it wanted (see voluērunt)

schola, ae, f., an upper school, school of rhetoric

> In contrast with *lūdus*, a *schola* is a school of rhetoric. It would correspond with an upper school, or the rhetoric stage. A *lūdus* corresponds to a lower school, or the grammar stage.

iūs, iūris, n., one's right or prerogative under the law; *plur. and here,* **rights**

> In contrast with *ius*, *lex* refers to the laws enacted by men, and the "legal machinery of a state" (OLD).

Colōniae Novae Angliae

ad + acc., here, *according to, in accordance with*

> *Ad* has many meanings in Latin, as do most prepositions. Here, it denotes the correspondence to a standard, that is, the Scriptures. See entry in OLD, 34-39

praeceptum, ī, n., teaching, precept

scriptūrae, ārum, f. pl., the Scriptures

Bostoniēnsis, e, adj., of Boston

> Compare to the local adjective in chapter 9, **Massachusettēnsis.**

litterae, ārum, f. pl., literature

Graecus, a, um, adj., Greek

RESPONDĒ LATĪNĒ:

1. Quis colōniam Puritanōrum in Novam Anglicam dēdūxit?

2. Quid est nomen illae colōniae?

3. Quis est Iohannes Winthrop?

4. Quid Iohanns Cotton condidit?

Quis – who?   Quid – what?

CAPUT XI

4/16/09

Rubra Insula
MDCXXXVI A.D.

Iam Rogerus Gulielmī et scholae Salem colōniam

reliquērant. Terram ab Indigeniīs emērant et novam colōniam

condidērant. Hanc terram "Rubram Insulam" appellābunt, quod

humus est ruber. Ibi omnēs lībertātem dē religiōne habēbunt.

Interim in eōdem oppidō Anna Hutchinson etiam

doctrinās et traditiōnēs colōniae provocāvit. Ea pastōrēs et

sermonēs male trādūxit. Anna vēram religiōnem esse "interiorem

lūcem" persōnae sine pastōribus aut praeceptīs dēclārāvit. Iohannes

Rubra Insula

Winthrop et ducēs Annam excommunicāvērunt. Ea et scholae

etiam ad Rubram Insulam movērunt et aliam novam colōniam

condidērunt.

      Posteā Rogerus ad Britanniam nāvigāvit. Chartam prō

novā colōniā rogāvit. Ante redībit, Indigenae Annam et familiam

necāverint.

Rubra Insula

GLOSSARY & NOTES:

Rubra Insula, f. Rhode Island

> This territory was named "Roodt Eylandt", which means "red island" in the Natives' tongue, for the red earth along the shoreline. Later, the name was changed to Rhode Island when the territory came under British rule.

Rogerus Gulielmī, m. Roger Williams

schola, ae, f. school; followers

> In addition to meaning school, this word may also refer to the followers, school, or sect of a philosopher and his teaching. "**clamābant omnēs philosophōrum scholae,**" Cicero
> (cf. school of fish)

relinquō, relinquere, relīquī, relictum, to leave behined, abandon

emō, emere, emī, emptum, to buy

ruber, rubra, rubrum, adj., red

religiō, religiōnis, f., religion

eōdem oppidō = that same town (i.e. Salem).

> The demonstrative pronoun *idem, eadem, idem* is derived from the third person pronoun *is, ea, id,* and is declined similarly. The suffix *-dem* is added for special emphasis.

Anna Hutchinson, f., Ann Hutchinson

traditiō, traditiōnis, f., tradition

male, adv., badly, wrongly (compare to *malus*)

provocō, āre, āvī , ātum, to provoke

pastor, pastōris, m., shepherd; pastor

trādūcō, trādūcere, trādūxi, trāductum, to disgrace, dishonor, 'show up'

> Anne would hold "discussion groups" in her home during which she would criticize the pastor and leaders of the colony. Such discussions, particularly from a woman, were considered improper and unacceptable.

Rubra Insula

<u>interior, interius</u>, comparative adj., inner

    <u>interiorem</u> < interior, interius. Comparative adjectives decline in a manner very similar to 3rd declension adjectives (2 termination).

<u>lūx, lūcis</u>, f., light

<u>excommunicō, āre, āvī, ātum</u>, to excommunicate

<u>charta, ae</u>, f., charter

RESPONDĒ LATINĒ:

1. Ubī Rogerus et Anna colōniās condidērunt?

2. Quis Annam excommunicāvit? Cūr?

3. Cūr appellāmus illum locum "Rubram Insulam"?

Ubī – where?   Quis – who?   Cūr – why?

CAPUT XII

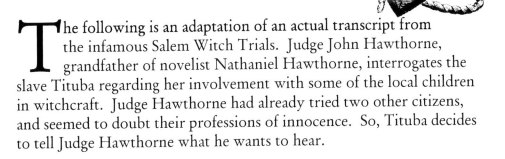

Interrogātiō
MDCXCII A.D.

T he following is an adaptation of an actual transcript from the infamous Salem Witch Trials. Judge John Hawthorne, grandfather of novelist Nathaniel Hawthorne, interrogates the slave Tituba regarding her involvement with some of the local children in witchcraft. Judge Hawthorne had already tried two other citizens, and seemed to doubt their professions of innocence. So, Tituba decides to tell Judge Hawthorne what he wants to hear.

<u>Hawthorne</u>: Daemonemne numquam vīdistī ?

<u>Tituba</u>: Daemon ad mē vēnit et mē eī servīre iussit . . . .

<u>Hawthorne</u>: Quale officium?

<u>Tituba</u>: Iniūria līberōrum; erat spectrum et dixit, "necā līberōs."

<u>Hawthorne</u>: Quid est hoc spectrum?

<u>Tituba</u>: Modo formam porcī habet, modo formam magnī canis.

Interrogātiō

Hawthorne: Quid tibi dixistī?

Tituba: Niger canis dixit, "servī mihi," sed dixī, "timeō."

Hawthorne: Quid eī dixistī ?

Tituba: Servīre tibi nōn optō. Deinde dixit, "male tibi nocēbō," et iam fōrmam hominis habet.

Hawthorne: Cūr nocte ad casam Thomae īvistī et infantī eius nocuistī?

Tituba: Mē trahunt et mē īre cōgunt . . .

Hawthorne: Quōmodo īvistī?

Tituba: In baculīs āvehimur et mox advenimus.

Hawthorne: Cūr tuō dominō nōn nārravistī?

Tituba: Timuī. Dixērunt,"tuum caput dētruncābimus, sī narrābis."

Interrogātiō

GLOSSARY & NOTES:

interrogātiō, interrogātiōnis, f., interrogation, cross-examination

daemon, daemonis, m., devil

serviō, servīre (+ dative), to serve, to be a slave to

qualis, quale, interrogative adj., what kind of

> This interrogative adjectives declines similarly to 3rd declension adjectives of two terminations (see ch. 3, LFC Primer C). [See AG 151]

spectrum, ī, n. apparition

> cf. *spectō, spectāre, spectāvī, spectātum*

quis, quid, interrogative pronoun/adj., who, what

modo . . . modo = sometimes . . . sometimes

porcus, ī, m. hog, pig

niger, nigra, nigrum, adj. black

noceō, nocēre, nocuī, nocitum (+dat.), to harm

cūr, interrogative adv. why

nocte, ablative of time when = at night < nox, noctis, f. night

infans, infantis, m/f., small child

cōgō, cōgere, coēgī, coactum, to force

quōmodo, interrogative adv., how, in what way

baculum, ī, n. stick

āvehimur = we ride away < āvehō, āvehere, āvexī, āvectum, to carry away

> This is the passive form of the verb **āvehere**. The literal translation would be "we are being carried away."

tuus, a, um, adj. your

dētruncō, āre, āvī, ātum, to cut off, behead

> *dētruncrāre* < *dē* (from) + *truncus, ī* (trunk, human body). Thus this verb literally means to cut off or strip (*truncāre*) the head from (*dē*) the body.

sī, conj., if

Interrogātiō

Nota Bene: Years later Judge Hawthorne made a public apology for his involvement in the witch trials and repented for making grievous errors.

RESPONDĒ LATĪNĒ:

1. Quid Tituba vīdit?

2. Qualem formam spectrum habuit?

3. Cūr Tituba timuit?

4. Crēdisne fābulam Titubae? Cūr aut nōn cūr?

Quid – what	qualem – what kind of
cūr – why	aut – or
Minime – no	ita vero – yes

CAPUT XIII

Līberī in Americanīs Colōniīs

MDCXX – MDCCXXXIII A.D.

Multī incolae in fundīs habitant. Sunt pauca oppida. Omnēs

līberī quī in colōniīs habitant labōrāre dēbent. In fundīs, puerī

patrēs arborēs caedere, agrōs arāre, et animalia cūrāre adiuvant.

Puellae mātrēs coquere, vaccās mulgēre, hortum cūrāre, et vestēs

candēlāsque facere adiuvant. Haec bona in oppidum portant. Ibi

cum aliīs colōnīs commūtant. Magnae nāvēs interdum haec bona

trāns mare portant.

Paucī līberī ad lūdum eunt, quod lūdī et librī sunt carī et

remōtī. Necesse est etiam labōrāre in fundō. Multī parentēs līberōs

legere scrībereque Bibliīs docent.

Cum nōn labōrant, līberī saepe pilā lūdunt, arborēs

ascendunt, aut pūpās faciunt. Spectāre spectācula pūpārum amant.

Circus interdum venit. Deinde līberī ferōs et fūnambulōs spectāre

possunt. Visne habitāre in colōniās?

Līberī in Americanīs Colōniīs

GLOSSARY & NOTES:

incola, ae, m., inhabitant, colonist

> Whereas *colōnus* was used by the Romans in reference to settlers coming from a foreign land to establish a colony, *incola* was used for their descendents who continued to inhabit it. Henceforth *incola* will refer to the American colonists who are by and large the descendents of the original settlers *(colōnus)*.

fundus, ī, m., farm

caedō, caedere, cecīdī, caesum, to chop down, cut down

coquō, coquere, coxī, coctum, to cook

vacca, ae, f., cow

> The word "vaccine" is derived from this Latin word for cow. Vaccinia was initially the viral agent for cowpox. When vaccinia was given to humans it provided protection against the illness.

mulgeō, mulgēre, mulsī, mulsum, to milk

candelāsque = candelās + que (and)

> The latter word, *-que,* is an enclitic. Enclitics are words which do not stand on their own but attach themselves to the end of the following word. An example of an enclitic in English would be the conjunction 'n.'
>
> (i.e. – bacon 'n' eggs, salt 'n' pepper)

candela, ae, f., candle

haec bona, n.pl., substantive adjective (an adjective representing a noun) = these goods

commūtō, āre, āvī, ātum, to trade (with cum + abl.)

liber, librī, m., book

necesse est = it is necessary

parens, parentis, m/f., parent

legō, legere, lēgī, lectum, to read

Biblia, -ōrum, n.pl., the Bible

> This word is always plural in form, but translated as singular. Think of a single Bible which consists of several books *(biblia)*.

> i.e. – the books of the Bible: Genesis, Proverbs, Matthew, etc.

pila, ae, f., ball

ascendō, ascendere, ascendī, ascensum, to climb

pūpa, ae, f., doll, puppet

spectāculum, ī, n., show, entertainment

circus, ī, m. circle, (best translated here as 'circus')

> The original meaning of this word was simply 'circle.' It then came to be associated with race tracks and other circular places for games and entertainment. Our modern Circus is derived from these.

fūnambulus, ī, m., tight rope walker

> This fun word is derived from *fūnāle* (rope) + *ambulāre* (to walk).

visne, vis + ne = do you wish/want? < irreg. *volō, velle* – to wish, want

> See the above note regarding enclitics.

JULIA
HULSANDER

Līberī in Americānīs Colōniīs

RESPONDĒ LATĪNĒ:

1. Quid puerī in fundīs faciunt?

2. Quid puellae faciunt?

3. Quōmodo līberī lūdunt?

4. Visne habitāre in colōniās?

Quid faciunt – what did they do?
Quōmodo – how, in what way?
Minime – no!   ita vero – yes!

CAPUT XIV

Fābula Agricolae
c. MDCCXL A.D.

Herī in agrīs labōrābam. Subitō, nūntius ad fundum

equitāvit et clāmāvit, "Gorgius Whitefield hodiē in oppidō

praedicābit." Statim ad casam cucurrī et uxorī clāmāvī, "Festīnā,

parā īre! Festīnā, aut sērō adveniēmus!" Et ego et uxor illum

equum equitāvimus. Cum erat dēfessus, iuxtā eum cucurrī.

Procul magnam nūbem, altam suprā arborēs, spectāvimus.

Eam esse nebulam flūminis putāvī. Sed erat pulvis multōrum

equōrum et carrōrum. Omnēs ad oppidum festīnābant. Cum

Fābula Agricolae

tandem advēnimus, duodecim milia pasuum equitāverāmus et

nullum virum, quī in agrīs labōrābat, vīderam. Omnēs audīre

sermōnēs huius virī volēbant. Deinde vertī et magnum flūmen,

plēnam cymbārum, et rīpam, plēnam turbārum exspectantium,

vīdī. Omnēs praesentiam Deī sitiēbant. Cum tandem Gorgius

praedicābat, deinde Spīritus Deī inter eōs flāvit, et corda populōrum

mūtāvit.

Fābula Agricolae

GLOSSARY & NOTES:

herī, adv., yesterday

subitō, adv., suddenly

equitō, āre, āvī, ātum, to ride (a horse)

hodiē, adv., today

praedicō, āre, āvī, ātum, to preach

statim, adv., immediately

et . . . et = both . . . and

aut, conj., or

sērō, adv., late

illum equum equitāvimus, the narrator and his wife rode double upon "that horse"

procul, adv., from a distance

nūbēs, nūbis, f., cloud

nebula, ae, f., fog

eam esse nebulam flūminis putāvī, Indirect Discourse. This construction which sometimes consists of a direct object followed by an infinitive + accusative is used with verbs of thinking or speaking. The literal translation would be, "I thought this to be the fog of the river." It may also be translated more loosely as, "I thought it was the fog of the river."

pulvis, pulveris, m., dust

quī, relative pronoun, nom., m., sing., who

volēbant = they were wanting, wishing < imperfect tense of *volō, velle*, to wish

cymba, ae, f., ferry boat, skiff

> This may also be spelled *cumbārum*.

turbārum exspectantium, genitive plural = of the waiting crowds

> exspectantium, present participle of *exspectāre* – The present participle is an adjective formed from a verb's stem. As with all adjectives, it must agree with the noun it modifies (*turbārum*) in case number and gender. [See AG,490]

Fābula Agricolae

praesentia, ae, f., presence
sitiō, sitīre, sitīvī, to thirst for

RESPONDĒ LATĪNĒ:

1. Quot milia pasuum agricola equitāvit?

2. Quis in oppidum praedicābit?

3. Cūr multī populī eum audīre volēbant?

4. Quis corda populōrum mūtat?

Quis – who?   Quot – how many?   Cūr?

CAPUT XV

Mercatūra cum Angliā
c. MDCCL A.D.

Novum Eboracum multās nāvēs ad Occidentalēs

Indiās cum frūmentīs, farīnīs, crustulīs, lignīs, butyrīs,

piscibus, et aliīs bonīs mittit. Multae nāvēs Bostoniam

in Novā Angliā cum frūmentīs et farīnīs eunt. Deinde

carnēs, butyrōs, aliōs piscēs, et alia bona ad Occidentalēs

Indiās portant.

Philadelphia magnam mercatūram cum aliīs colōniīs

et Angliā, Hiberniā, Lusitaniā, et Australī Americā facit.

Nulla nāvis autem praeter Anglicās portum Philadelphiae

intrāre potest.

Magna copia sēminis līnī simul cum multīs nāvibus, quae in Americā aedificāmus, quotannīs ad Hiberniam it. Interdum decem nāvēs in ūnō annō sēmen līnī ad Hiberniam portant! America frūmenta et farīnās ad Lusitaniam mittit. Interdum frūmenta ad Hispāniam mittit. Tōta pecūnia autem, quae hae aliēnae terrae mercatūrae dant, ad Angliam īre dēbent.

Mercatūra cum Angliā

GLOSSARY & NOTES:

<u>Novum Eboracum</u>, n., New York

<u>Occidentalēs Indiae</u>, f., West Indies

<u>farīna, ae</u>, f., flour

<u>crustulum, ī</u>, n., biscuit, cookie

<u>lignum, ī</u>, n., wood, timber

<u>butyrum, ī</u>, n., butter

<u>Bostoniam</u>, accusative of place to which = to Boston

> The names of towns, small islands, and the nouns *domus* and *rus* do not use a Latin preposition for references to place. The accusative is used without a preposition to show motion toward a place, and ablative is used without a preposition to motion away from.

<u>carno, carnis</u>, f., meat

<u>Philadelphia, ae</u>, f., Philadelphia

<u>mercatūram . . . facit</u> = it trades.

> This phrase is a classical idiomatic expression meaning that may simply be translated as "it trades". The literal translation would be "it makes trade".

<u>Hibernia, ae</u>, f., Ireland

<u>Lusitania, ae</u>, f., Portugal

<u>austrālis, e</u>, adj., Southern

> The southern continent, Australia, gets its name from this Latin word. *Australis* (southern, south) is itself derived from *Auster*, the Roman name for the South Wind.

<u>portum</u>, acc., sing., masc., < portus, portūs, m., port

<u>nullus . . . portum Philadelphiae intrāre potest</u>, This prohibition against foreign ships entering American ports was part of the Navigation Acts.

<u>semen linī</u>, n., flaxseed (literally "seed of flax")

> Flax, widely cultivated plant having blue flowers, produces

linseed oil and its fibers are used to produce a textile also referred to as flax. Flaxseed (or linseed) was exported in great quantities to Ireland. Some believed it was because the flaxseed in Ireland could not produce good seed for crops. Others seemed to think the Irish preferred to make use of the plant before it was ripe and thus unable to produce seed for planting.

in ūnō annō, ablative of time within which. This construction is typically used without a preposition. However, it is sometimes preceded by the preposition *in* for emphasis. *"in* one year" [AG, 424]

quae, relative pronoun referring to *pecūniae*, nom., pl., fem., which

RESPONDĒ LATĪNĒ:

1. Quid nāvēs ad Occidentālēs Indiās portant?

2. Quandō nāvēs Philadelphiae eunt?

3. Quis intrāre portum Philadelphiae potest?

4. Cui aliēnae terrae pecūniam mercatūrae dant?

Quid – what? Quandō – to where? Quis – who? Cui – to whom?

CAPUT XVI

Bellum contrā Galliās Indigenāsque

MDCCLIV - MDCCLXIII A.D.

Britannia contrā Galliam in Americā pugnābat. Multī

Indigenae Galliam adiuvābant, quod Brittanicōs incolās excēdere

cupiēbant. Aliī Indigenae autem Brittanicōs adiuvābant.

Imperātor Brittanicus, nōmine Braddock, iam ad Castellum

Duquesne prōcēdit. Illum castellum esse infirmum et male parātum

scit. Per magnās silvās autem prōcēdere necesse est. Hae silvae sunt

plēnae Indigenārum, sociōrum Galliae. Vasingtonius perīculum

sentit et Imperātōrem monet, "Carrōs et gravia tormenta relinquere

Bellum contrā Galliās Indigenāsque

dēbēmus; celeriter prōcēdere dēbēmus!" Sed Imperātor nōn audiet.

"Istī Indigenae Brittanicās copiās capere nōn possunt," respondet.

Subito, multae arborēs in silvā multōs Indigenās aperiunt,

quī multās sagittās iaciunt. Magnā cum clāmōre mīlitēs et

Indigenae in proeliō saevō conveniunt. Indigenae superbiam

Imperātōris punient; eum vulnerant et mox perībit. Vasingtonium

vulnerāre nōn possunt, quī copiās incitat. Multī Britannicī ducēs

cadunt et infēlīcēs copiae recēdunt. Britannicī neque ad castellum

advenient neque id capient.

Bellum contrā Galliās Indigenāsque

GLOSSSARY & NOTES:

excēdō, excēdere, excessī, excessum, to go away, leave

Castellum Duquesne = Fort Duquesne

prōcēdō, prōcēdere, prōcessī, prōcessum, to proceed, (mil.) advance

necesse est (+ infinitive) = it is necessary to _____

Indigenārum, sociōrum Galliae, The noun *sociōrum* serves in apposition to the preceding noun *Indigenārum*, and is therefore placed in the same case.

Vasingtonius, ī, m., Washington (George Washington)

tormenta, ōrum, n. pl., artillery

dēbēmus + infinitive = best translated here as "we must"

> *Debēmus* + infinitive – The verb *dēbēre* is commonly translated as 'to owe, ought' and is followed by a complementary infinitive (an infinitive which completes the intended meaning of the verb).

> i.e. *prōcēdere dēbēmus* = we ought to advance

> It may also be translated more emphatically as 'must,' still taking a complementary infinitive.

> i.e. *prōcēdere dēbēmus* = we must advance

Istī Indigenae, The demonstrative pronoun/adjective *iste, ista, istud* was often used by the Romans with a sense of contempt upon the person or object referred to. Here the demonstrative is used to illustrate General Braddock's feeling of contempt toward the Natives of America. He did not feel "those natives" would be any match for disciplined British troops.

sagitta, ae, f., arrow

quī, pronoun, nom., masc., pl., who

proelium, ī, n., battle

superbia, ae, f., pride

incitō, āre, āvī, ātum, to urge on

recēdō, recēdere, recessī, recessum, to retreat

> *excēdere, prōcēdere, recēdere* – This trio of verbs serve as a demonstration of compound verbs in Latin, which are reviewed in chapter 15 of LFC, Primer C. The meaning of the verb *cēdere* (to go, move) is changed slightly with the addition of the prefixes *ex, prō,* and *re.*

Bellum contrā Galliās Indigenāsque

ex (out of) + *cēdere* = to go out of, depart, leave

prō (before) + *cēdere* = to go forward, advance

re (back) + *cēdere* = to go back, retreat

neque . . . neque = neither . . . nor

RESPONDĒ LATĪNĒ :

1. Cūr multī Indignae prō Galliā pugnābant?

2. Quis est Imperātor Brittanicōrum?

3. Quis Imperātōrem dē Indigenīs mōnet?

4. Quis hoc proelium vincit?

Cūr – why?   Quis – who?

CAPUT XVII

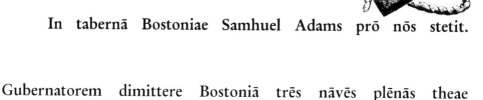

Thea Convivium
MDCCLXXIII A.D.

In tabernā Bostoniae Samhuel Adams prō nōs stetit.

Gubernatorem dimittere Bostoniā trēs nāvēs plēnās theae

rogāverāmus. Sed, cum silentiō modo respondit. Samhuel dixit,

"nihil plūs facere possumus!" haec verba erant signum. Magnā cum

clāmōre ē tabernā festīnāvimus. Faciēs carbōne pinximus et secūrēs

cēpimus. Nōs, nunc manus Indigenārum, ad nāvēs processimus.

Manus prīmam nāvem conscendit. Magistrum iussī, "fer mihi

candelās et clāvēs nāvis." Eās tulit et rogāvit, "nocēbitisne nāvī?"

Thea Convivium

Respondī, "nihil praeter theam nocēbimus."

Nox erat, sed portus erat lux quasi diēs. Multae lanternae nostram labōrem apuērunt. Cistās theae sustulimus, eās secūre effrēgimus, et eās in portum iecimus. Mox aliī virī, cīvēs Bostoniae, advēniērunt et adiuvāvērunt. Omnēm theam in illā nāve dēlēvimus.

Postea secundam nāvem conscendimus, tum tertiam nāvem. CCCXLII cistās theae dēlēvimus. Postea, nāvēs mundāvimus et omnia in aptō locō posuimus. Omnia sine sonō sine pugnā fēcimus, dum Britannicae nāvēs spectāvērunt.

Thea Convivium

GLOSSARY & NOTES:

thea, ae, f., tea

> The Romans did not drink tea and therefore had no name for the beverage. This is taken from the Latinized botanical name of the Chinese tea plant, *thea sinensis*.

convīvium, ī, n., social gathering; party

gubernatorem, Governor Hutchinson, the king's chief officer in the colony of Massachusettes. Governor Hutchinson had given the "rebels" three days to allow the ships to unload their cargo peacefully or it would be unloaded under fire of cannon. Samuel Adams and others tried during these three days to diplomatically arrive at a solution with the governor. The tea party was held on the evening of the third day.

dimitto, dimittere, dimīsī, dimissum, to send away

Bostoniā = from Boston

> The names of towns, small islands, and the nouns *domus* and *rus* do not use a Latin preposition for references to place. The ablative is used without a preposition to show motion from a place, and accusative is used without a preposition to motion toward.

modo, adv., only

plūs, adv., more

"nihil plūs facere possumus!" – Samuel Adams' statements was actually, "We are able to do nothing more to save our country." Meaning that the time for words and diplomacy had come to an end.

faciēs, acc., fem., pl. < faciēs, ēī, f., face

carbō, carbōnis, m., charcoal

pingō, pingere, pinxī, pictum, to paint

secūris, securis, f., hatchet

manus, nom., fem., sing., < manus, manūs, f. hand, band

conscendō, conscendere, conscendī, conscensum, to board (a ship)

fer, singular imperative of *ferre*

clāvis, clāvis, f., key

portus, nom., masc., sing., < portus, portūs, m., port, harbor

Thea Convivium

<u>quasi</u>, conj., as if

<u>diēs</u>, nom., fem., sing. < diēs, diēī, f., day

<u>noster, nostra, nostrum</u>, adj., our

<u>effringō, effringere, effrēgī, effractum</u>, to break open

<u>dēleō, dēlēre, dēlēvī, dēlētum</u>, to destroy

<u>mundō, āre, āvī, ātum</u>, to clean

<u>dum</u>, adv., while

<u>dum Britannicae nāvēs spectāvērunt</u> – British war ships were actually stationed around the Boston harbor the night of the tea party. While they witnessed the events, they never once threatened or fired upon the colonists.

RESPONDĒ LATĪNĒ:

1. Ubī erat Samhuel Adams?

2. Quid vir in faciē posuit?

3. Quot cistās dēlēvērunt?

4. Quid in cistīs erat?

Ubī – where?   Quid – what?   Quot – how many?

CAPUT XVIII

Prīma Congressiō Continens
MDCCLXXIV A.D.

Britannia erat īrāta propter Theam Convīvium. Ita Dēcrēta

Intolerābilia creāvit. Ūna lex portum Bostoniēnsem clausit. Alia

lex potentiam gubernatoris Massechuttensis crēvit, sed illam

cīvitātis dēcrēvit. Tōtae colōniae erant īrātae et sollicitae. Aliī

bellum gerēre cupīvērunt, aliī id timuērunt.

Colōniae Prīmam Congressiōnem Continentem creāvērunt.

Responsum prō Americā erat officium Congressiōnis. Congressiō

Dēclārātionem Iūrum Iniūriārumque scripsit. Haec Dēclārātiō

Prīma Congressiō Continens

fidēlitātem Rēgī affirmāvit. Rēgem Dēcrēta Intolerābilia tollere et

potentiam Brittanicam in Americā termināre rogāvit. Congressiō

etiam incolās mercatūram cum Brittaniā nōn facere iussit donec Rēx

dēcrēta sustulerit. Prīma Congressiō Continens pacem cum Rēge et

Brittaniā cupīvit, sed bellum vītāre nōn potuit.

GLOSSARY & NOTES:

<u>congressiō, congressiōnis</u>, f., congress (lit. meeting, conference)

<u>continens, continentis</u>, adj., continental (lit. mainland, continent)

<u>dēcrētum, ī</u>, n., decree, act

<u>intolerābilis, e</u>, adj., intolerable

<u>Bostoniēnsem, Massechuttensis</u> - Adding the ending –*ēnsis* to a place name is the common and classical way of creating its adjectival form. These same adjectives are used in chapters 9 and 10.

<u>potentia, ae</u>, f., power

<u>dēcrescō, dēcrescere, dēcrēvī, dēcrētum</u>, to diminish, decrease

<u>aliī . . . aliī</u> = some . . . others

<u>responsum, ī</u>, n., response

<u>Dēclārātionem Iūrum Iniūriārumque</u> = Declaration of Rights and Grievances

<u>fidēlitās, fidēlitātis</u>, f., loyalty, fidelity

<u>terminō, āre, āvī, ātum</u>, to limit

<u>mercatūram . . . facere</u> – classical idiom, "to trade" (lit. to make trade). This same expression is used in chapter 15.

<u>donec</u>, conj., until

Prīma Congressiō Continens

RESPONDĒ LATĪNĒ:

1. Cūr Britannia erat īrāta?

2. Cūr colōniae erant īrātae et sollicitae?

3. Quid erat officium Congressiōnis?

4. Quid Declaratiō Iūrum Iniuriārumque dixit?

5. Potuēruntne Congressiō bellum vītāre?

Cūr – why?
Quid – what?
Minime – no
ita vero - yes

CAPUT XIX

Equitatio
MDCCLXXV A.D.

Est obscūra nox, nox fatī. Iosephus Warren, medicus

et Fīlius Lībertātis, amīcō nārrat, "consilium Britannicōrum

invēnimus. Marī vēnient. Festīnā, monē incolās!" Celeriter Paulus

Revere in nōctem currit. Mox ad Antīquam Septentrionalem

Ecclēsiam advenit. Cum erat puer, Paulus saepe tintinnabula

eius tractāverat. Iam est nullus sonus. Dum Rubrae Togae suprā

dormiunt, aedituum duās lanternās in altā fenestrā pōnere iubet.

Illae lanternae multōs virōs dē consiliō Britannicō monēbunt.

Equitatio

Statim, Paulus suum equum, Spadicem Fōrmam, per cīvitātem

equitat. Somnus incolās in casīs tenuit. Sed iam fortis nūntius eōs

clārīs verbīs excitat, "Britannicī veniunt! Britannicī veniunt!"

Virī ē lectibus saliunt, parātī mōmentō tempōris. Mox pugnāverint,

necāverint, et perierint. Mox America et Britannia bellum gerent.

Equitatio

GLOSSARY & NOTES:

equitatio, equitationis, f. horseride

obscūrus, a, um, adj., dark

Iosephus Warren – This great patriot was part of a secret network known as the Sons of Liberty (*Fīlius Lībertātis*), who supported the rebellion against England. He is also known as the Martyr of Bunker Hill. Although a physician, and therefore excused from battle, he fought at the Battle of Bunker Hill and gave his life in order to hold off the British enabling others to retreat.

marī, ablative of means = by sea

The ablative case is used to express the means by which something is accomplished. The British will travel by means of the sea as opposed to travel by land.

celeriter, adv., quickly

septemtriōnālis, e, adj. northern, north

This adjective was derived from the Latin word *septemtriōnēs*, the name for the seven stars near the North Pole that belong to the constellation *Ursa Maior* (the Big Bear). The Romans referred to the constellations of *Ursa Maior* and *Ursa Minor* (the Little Bear) together as the *Triōnēs*.

Antīqua Septentrionalis Ecclesia, = Old North Church

tintinnabula tractaverat = he had rung the bells

As a boy, Paul Revere with his family attended the Old North Church. He and many of his friends served the church by ringing the bells for services and other special occasions. He must have been very well acquainted with the famous bell tower. *Tintinnabula* is a great example of onomatopoeia also used by the Romans.

Rubrae Togae = red coats

On account of the Quartering Act, granting British soldiers quarter, or dwelling, wherever they chose, some Red Coats were asleep upstairs in the Sexton's lodgings when Paul arrived with his orders.

suprā, here *suprā* is used as an adverb

aedituus, ī, m., sexton (church attendant)

88

Equitatio

In ancient Rome this would have been the title given to the temple attendant. Robert Newman, a patriot, was the sexton at this time. Upon Revere's command, it was he who placed the lanterns in the bell tower window.

Spadix Fōrma = Brown Beauty, Paul Revere's horse

equitō, āre, āvī, ātum, to ride (a horse)

excitō, āre, āvī, ātum, to wake, to arouse

lectō, lectis, f., bed

saliō, salīre, salīvī, salitum, to leap, jump

mōmentō temporis, ablative of time within which = in a minute (lit. in a moment of time)

bellum gerere, classical idiom = to wage war

RESPONDĒ LATĪNĒ:

1. Quis est Iosephus Warren?

2. Quot lanternae sunt in fenestrā?

3. Quī in casā aedituī dormiunt?

4. Quem Revere equitat?

5. Quid Revere clāmat?

Quis – who
Quot – how many
Quī – who (pl.)
Quem – (acc.) whom
Quid - what

CAPUT XX

Collis
MDCCLXXV A.D.

Ūnā diē calidā Iuniō, Iosephus Warren amīcam, cuius vir ad

Theam Convīvium adfuerat et in colle pugnābit, vīsitat. "Venī, mea

puella parva," dicit "calicem vīnī mēcum bibis, nam crās ad collem

ībō et numquam recēdam."

Postrīdiē ad collem extrā Bostoniam procēdit. In colle

hōc est parvus manus virōrum, quī collem et Bostoniam contrā

Brittanicum exercitum dēfendent. Virī adventum amātī medicī

gaudent. Apud eōs est Petrus Salem, lībertus. Petrus servus fuerat, sed dominus eum līberāvit quod Petrus pugnāre prō Americā

cupīvit. Nunc Petrus, Iosephus, et aliī collem contrā magnum

exercitum Britannicum dēfendere parant.

Britannicus impetus incipit. Multī mīlitēs ad collem

prōcēdunt. Dux manūs clāmat, "Nolite iaculārī dōnec albam

partem oculōrum vidētis!" Incolae Britannicōs bis repellunt. Multī

mīlitēs Brittanicī cadunt. Sed incolae parvum pulverem tormentīs

habent; recēdere necesse est.

Brittanicus dux, Iohannes Pitcairn, tertium impetum incitat,

"dies est nostrī!" clāmat. Subito, Pitcairn cadit. Petrus eum necāvit. Brittanicī stupent; multī Americanī recēdere possunt. Sed

Iosephus perit dum sociōs dēfendit. Post proelium mīlitēs Novae

Angliae et Imperātor Vasingtonius mortem Iosephī lūgent et

virtūtem Petrī laudant.

Collis

GLOSSARY & NOTES:

Collis, Bunker Hill or Breed's Hill. While the infamous battle is known as the Battle of Bunker Hill, most of the action took place on nearby Breed's Hill.

Ūnā diē calidā Iūniō, ablative of time when

Iosephus Warren, Joseph Warren first appears in ch. 19. Dr. Warren is best known for the role he played in the Midnight Ride of Paul Revere. However, he is also known by the epitaph, "The Martyr of Bunker Hill." A man of little fighting experience, he volunteered to join the colonial troops in the defense of Boston, against the urgings of General Putnam. He was last seen defending the retreat of the colonists during the third and final British advance. Following the battle, his body was thrown in a mass grave by the British soldiers. Paul Revere later identified his friend's body by a dental filling which Revere, a silversmith, had made for him. His body was moved and is now marked by an honorable headstone.

amīcam, Betsy Palmer. Mrs. Palmer's husband had joined the Tea Party and would also fight at the Battle of Bunker Hill.

vīsitō, āre, āvī, ātum, to visit

calix, calicis, m., cup

mēcum = cum mē

numquam, adv., never

postrīdiē, adv., the next day, following day

amātus, a, um, adj., beloved

Petrus Salem, m., Peter Salem

> Peter Salem, so named for his first master's hometown of Salem, had been a slave all of his life. He was freed in return for his commitment to serve in the colonial army. Both American and British troops at different times during the Revolutionary War offered freedom to those slaves who would serve in their armies.

lībertus, ī, m., freedman (one who has been freed from slavery)

dēfendō, dēfendere, dēfendī, dēfensum, to defend, protect

impetus, ūs, m., attack, assault

incipiō, incipere, incēpī, inceptum, to begin, start

nolite iaculārī, negative imperative = do not fire!

Dux manūs, General Israel Putnam was the leader of the colonial army defending Breed's Hill and the author of this famous quote.

repellō, repellere, reppulī, repulsum, to drive back

tormentum, ī, n., artillery piece; best translated as "gun"

pulverem tormentīs = powder for guns, gun powder

> The American defense failed primarily due to the lack of gun powder and ammunition available to the colonial troops. Before giving up the hill in retreat, the Americans killed 40% of the attacking British forces; a huge blow to the British army.

Iohannes Pitcairn, m., John Pitcairn, Major in the British army

> Major John Pitcairn was the leader of the British ground forces attacking Breed's Hill. He was mortally wounded by Peter Salem during the third and final advance; an act for which Peter Salem was later rewarded by the soldiers of New England and praised by General Washington himself.

stupeō, stupēre, stupuī, to be stunned, stupefied

Nota Bene: *The Battle of Bunker's Hill*, painted by John Trumbull in 1786, depicts the death of Doctor and General Joseph Warren. In the right hand corner a black colonist can be seen with a raised gun. Many believe this to be Peter Salem. A portion of this painting is shown on History Card #20 of the Explorers to 1815 History Series by Veritas Press.

Collis

RESPONDĒ LATĪNĒ:

1. Quis est Iosephus Warren?

2. Quid est lībertus?

3. Cūr dominus Petrī eum līberāvit?

4. Cūr recēdere necesse est?

5. Quis est Iohannes Pitcairn?

Quis – who?   Quid – what?   Cūr?

CAPUT XXI

Dēclārātiō Lībertātis
MDCCLXXVI A.D.

Multī Americanī libellum, nomine Vulgārem Prūdentiam,

lēgerant. Aliī eum nōn amāvērunt, sed aliī lībertātem ā Brittaniā

cupiēbant. Iam Britannicus Rēx octodecim milia Germanicōs

manūs ad Americam mittit. Adventus eōrum multōs amāntēs

patriae terret. Igitur, necesse est iam affirmāre causam lībertātis;

necesse est subsidium Galliae obtinēre; necesse est dēclārāre

lībertātem Americae!

Americanī magistrātūs iuvenem Virginiae scrībere gravem

dēclārātiōnem rogant. Diū hic iuvenis, Thoma Jeffersonius, in

sōlitūdine scrībit. Verba magnā cum cūrā optat, nam ea cursum

populī constituent. Tandem, quartō diē Iūliī, Thoma et magistrātūs

Americanī Dēclārātiōnem Lībertātis populō et mundī dōnant. Haec

verba sunt nōn modo dēclārātiō lībertātis sed bellī.

Dēclārātiō Lībertātis

GLOSSARY & NOTES:

dēclārātiō, dēclārātiōnis, f., declaration, proclamation

lībertās, This word can be translated several different ways in this passage: freedom, independence, liberty

libellus, ī, m., little book

>This is the diminutive form of līber, and is best translated as 'little book'.

nomine = called

Vulgārem Prūdentiam, Common Sense by Thomas Paine. This pamphlet or "little book" on the topic of America's liberty stirred many Americans towards separation from England.

aliī . . . aliī = some . . . others

octodecim milia = eighteen thousand

Germanicōs manūs, King George III hired German mercenary troops, some of which were called Hessians, to aide the British during the Revolutionary War.

amāntes patriae = patriots (literally: lovers of their country)

igitur, adv., therefore

necesse est = it is necessary (This phrase is often followed by an infinitive.)

subsidium, ī, n., military support

obtineō, obtinēre, obtinuī, obtentum, to take hold of, possess (ob + tenēre)

Thoma Jeffersonius, m., Thomas Jefferson

>This is the Latinization which Francis Glass used in his *Vita Washingtonii*.

sōlitūdinō, sōlitūdinis, f., solitude, loneliness

quartō diē, ablative of time when = on the fourth day

mundus, ī, m., world, mankind

modo, adv., only

Dēclārātiō Lībertātis

NOTA BENE:

quartō diē Iūliī - This date appears in accordance with our modern calendar. The Roman calendar would have dated this event in history as *ante diem IV Nonās Iuliās* (four days before the Nones of July). The Romans had three regular holidays each month. The Kalends fell on the first day, the Nones on the fifth or seventh, and the Ides on the thirteenth or fifteenth. The Romans counted down to each of these holidays much like we count down to Christmas.

RESPONDĒ LATĪNĒ:

1. Unde Rēx Britannicus manūs mittit?

2. Cūr est neccese dēclārāre lībertātem?

3. Quid Thoma scrībit?

4. Cūr Thoma verba cum cūrā optāre dēbet?

Unde - from where?   Cūr - why?   Quid - what?

CAPUT XXII

Imperātor Gorgius Vasingtonius

MDCCLXXV - MDCCLXXXI A.D.

Ante erat magnus imperātor, Gorgius Vasingtonius erat

mētātor. Multa praedia in Virginiā et vicīnīs terrīs permensus erat.

Hic ūsus erat beneficium in Bellō contrā Galliās Indigenāsque.

Quod geōgraphiam illōrum collium, plānitiērum, et silvārum

cognōverat, multās pugnās vincere potuit. Propter illās victoriās

et ūsum in bellō, annō MDCCLCCV, Vasingtonius Summus

Imperātor omnium exercituum Americanōrum factus est.

Principiō, multa parva proelia vicit. Postea, Britannicī

Imperātor Gorgius Vasingtonius

iterum et iterum eum recēdere impulērunt. Hieme annī

MDCCLCCVI, Americanī erat dēfessī et dēspērātī. Tandem,

vicesimō sextō diē Decembris, Vasingtonius impetum iussit.

Exercitum trāns flūmen, nomine Delawar, dūxit. Americanī

Germanicum exercitum sēmisomnem dēprehendērunt. Nullī

Americanī perērunt, sed commeātūs, tela, et captivōs cēpērunt.

Americanus exercitus iterum flūmen trānsit et alium proelium

vicit. Iam, Britannicī recēdēbant. Hae victoriae Americanīs spem

dedērunt.

Imperātor Gorgius Vasingtonius

GLOSSARY & NOTES:

Gorgius Vasingtonius, m., George Washington

mētātor, mētātōris, m., surveyor

praedium, ī, n., estate

permensus erat, 3rd person, sing., pluperfect tense of *permētīrī*- he had surveyed

> This is a deponent verb, passive in form but active in meaning.

geōgraphia, ae, f., geography

summus, a, um, adj., highest, supreme

factus est, 3rd person, sing., perfect tense of irregular verb *fio*- he became

principiō = in the beginning

iterum, adv., again

impellō, impellere, impulī, impulsum, to force

despērātus, a, um, adj., hopeless, dispirited

vicesimō sextō, ablative of time when = on the twenty sixth

Delawar, The Delware River was the sight of Washington's famous crossing. The river was named for Governor De La Warr of Virginia (see chapter 7).

sēmisomnis, e, adj., half-asleep

> The continental army surprised the German, or more accurately Hessian, troops early on the morning of December 26th. They found the troops sleepy from several nights of extended watch due to small raids by the colonial army. In fact, Commander Rall had to be awoken twice by his aide before realizing he was under attack.

dēprehendō, dēprehendere, dēprehendi, dēprehensum, to surprise

telum, ī, n., weapon

captivus, ī, m., prisoner (of war)

hae victoriae, Washington again crossed the Delaware to wage battles both at Princeton and again at Trenton. Following these successes, the British army pulled completely out of New Jersey; and the world gained a new respect for the Continental Army.

Imperātor Gorgius Vasingtonius

NOTA BENE:

vicesimō sextō diē Decembris – This date appears in accordance with our modern calendar. The Roman calendar would have dated this event in history as *ante diem IX Kalendās Ianuariās* (nine days before the Kalends of January). See the note regarding the Roman Calendar in the previous chapter, Dēclārātiō Lībertātis.

RESPONDĒ LATĪNĒ:

1. Quōmodo ūsus mētātōris erat beneficium?

2. Quandō Vasingtonius Imperātor Americanī exercituum factus est?

3. Quotiens Americanī flūmen trānsīvērunt?

Quōmodo – how?
Quando – when?
Quotiens – how many times?

CAPUT XXIII

Difficilis Hiems
MDCCLXXVII – MDCCLXXVIII A.D.

Hōc annō Americanī saepe ante Britannicum exercitum

recesserant. Vasingtonius Fabianam rem mīlitarem optāvit.

Imperātor aperta proelia contrā hostēs nōn pugnāvit. Potius parva

proelia et receptūs optavit. Quidam eum dubitābant.

Nunc Americanus exercitus in valle iuxta Philadelphiam

hiberna castra pōnunt. Mīlitēs frigidī, iēiūnī, et nudī pedibus

adveniunt. Nova domus eōrum est vallis plēna nivisque arborum.

Mīlitēs multa tuguria aedificāre dēbent. Thoma Paine scrībit, "erat

Difficilis Hiems

quasi familia castorum, omnēs sunt occupatī, aliī tigna ferunt, aliī

lutum, et cētera eōs confīgunt." Dum labōrant, cantant, "Nullus

pānis! nulla carnis!" Paucī virōrum etiam suōs calceōs antīquōs

coquunt et edunt!

Vasingtonius dolōrem virōrum lūget. Multās epistulās

Congressiōnī mittit. Cibōs, vestēs, et commeatūs rogat. Imperātor

ipse in tentōriō apud virōs habitat. In casam nōn movēbit dōnec

tōtī mīlitēs in tuguriīs habitāre possunt. Est longa et difficilis

hiems. Sed Vasingtonius respectum et fidem mīlitum vincit.

Difficilis Hiems

GLOSSARY & NOTES:

hōc annō, ablative of time within which = "in this year"

Fabianam rem mīlitarēm = Fabian military tactic (literally: the military thing of Fabius)

> Fabius Maximus served as dictator of Rome during the Second Punic War. He used delaying tactics against the army of Hannibal. The constant retreat caused Hannibal, far from home, to use up men and supplies. Eventually he had to leave for home. Washington had studied his Roman military history!

apertus, a, um, adj. open

potius, adv. rather, instead

receptus, ūs, m., retreat (military)

vallis, vallis, f., valley (specifically: Valley Forge)

hibernus, a, um, adj. winter

castra pōnere = to pitch camp (military phrase)

frigidus, a, um, adj. cold

iēiūnus, a, um, adj. hungry

nudī pedibus, best translated = with bare (naked) feet

> This phrase is an example of the ablative of respect. It is literally translated as, "the soldiers naked in respect to their feet."

nix, nivis, f., snow

tugurium, ī, n. cabin

Thoma Paine, Thomas Paine, author of Common Sense, served as the first war correspondent. He traveled with Washington's army writing his observations for the newspapers. More than once his words revived the hope and courage of Americans.

castor, castoris, m., beaver

occupatus, a, um, adj., busy

tignum, ī, n. log

lutum, ī, n., mud

confīgō, configere, confixī, confixum, to bind together

Difficilis Hiems

<u>pānis, pānis</u>, f., bread

<u>carnis, carnis</u>, f., meat

<u>calceus, ī</u>, m., shoe

<u>ipse, ipsa, ipsum</u>, intensive adj., himself

<u>tentōrium, ī</u>, n. tent

<u>respectus, ūs</u>, m., respect

Washington's men witnessed the sacrifice of their leader and his tireless efforts on their behalf during this very difficult winter. Because of Washington's service to his men, he gained their respect and trust.

RESPONDĒ LATĪNĒ:

1. Quid est Fabianam rem mīlitarem?

2. Cūr quidam Vasingtonium dubitant?

3. Ubī hiberna castra pōnunt?

4. Quōmodo Vasingtonius respectum et fidem vincit?

Quid – what?
Cūr – why?
Ubī – where?
Quōmodo – how, in what way?

CAPUT XXIV

Proelium Eboracī Oppidī

MDCCLXXXI A.D.

Some women chose to join their husbands as they went off to war. They cooked for soldiers, mended clothing and blankets, some even manned the cannons. The following is based on testimony given by Susan Osborn, wife of soldier Aaron Osborn, who was present during the Battle of Yorktown.

Cum Eboracum Oppidum advēnī, magnam plānitiem inter

castellum et exercitum Americanum vīdī. Corpora Aethiopum

mortuum in plānitie iacuērunt. Multōs diēs postea clāmōrem

tormentōrum audivī. Deinde Americanī mīlitēs, etiam meus vir,

valla fōdērunt. Carnem, pānem, et coffeam Arabicam coxī et eōs in

vallum mīlitibus tulī. Ibi ego ob viam Imperātorī Vasingtoniō ivī.

Mē rogāvit, "Nōnne tū tormentī ictūs timēs?" Respondī, "Minime,

tormentum patibulum nōn fraudābit. Virī et pugnāre et fame

perīre nōn dēbent."

Nocte omne valla propioraque propiora castellō fōdērunt.

Dum fōdērunt, hostēs graviter iaculātus sunt. Subitō, prīmā

lūce, sonus tympanōrum Britannicōrum clāmōrem tormentōrum

reposuit. Deinde nostrī mīlitēs clāmāvērunt. "Quid est?" mīlitem

rogāvī. "Nōnne tū scīs?" respondit, "Britannicī sē trādidērunt! Nōs

vīcimus!"

Proelium Eboracī Oppidī

GLOSSARY & NOTES:

Eboracum Oppidum, n., Yorktown

> Compare to *"Novum Eboracum"* in chapter 15.

Aethiops, Aethiopis, m. blackman, Ethiopian

> During the siege of Yorktown, the British quickly ran low on food and supplies. Sadly, they prolonged their resistance by sending the black men, whose freedom they had promised in return for joining the British army, out of the fort. The men were caught between the American army and the British fort. It seemed that many starved to death there.

vir, best translated here as "husband"

fodiō, fodere, fōdī, fossum, to dig (compare to fossa)

coffea Arabica, f., coffee

ob viam ire, (+ dative) = to meet (literally "to go in the way")

nōnne, interrogative adv., are you not?, aren't you?

> This interrogative adverb is used to introduce a question that contains a negative and expects the answer *yes*.

ictus, ūs, m. blow

> **tormentī ictūs** = cannonballs or blows of the cannon

patibulum, ī, n. gallows

> The gallows, where someone would be hanged, were a method of execution often used for traitors, such as those rebelling against England.

fraudō, āre, āvī, ātum, to cheat

fame perire = to die by starvation, to starve

propiorus, a, um, adj. (+ dat.), nearer, closer

graviter, adv. heavily (compare to gravis)

iaculātus sunt = they fired < iaculor, iacularī, iaculatus sum, deponent verb – to fire

> Deponent verbs have passive endings, that you will learn later, but are translated as regular active verbs, the kind you know now.

Proelium Eboracī Oppidī

prīma lūce = at first light, dawn

tympanum, ī, n. drum

sē tradidērunt = they surrendered (literally, they gave themselves over)

> sē is another kind of pronoun meaning "themselves".

RESPONDĒ LATĪNĒ:

1. Cūr Susana cum exercitū erat?

2. Quōmodo Susana adiuvāvit?

3. Quid mīlitēs fecērunt?

4. Quid sonus tympanōrum significat?

Cūr – why?
Quōmodo - how, in what way?
Quid – what?
Quid significant – what does it mean?

CAPUT XXV

Constitūtiō Cīvitātium Americae Foederātārum

MDCCLXXXVII A.D.

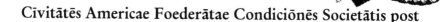

Cīvitātēs Americae Foederātae Condiciōnēs Societātis post

bellum adoptāverant. Patriam autem nōn bene administrāvērunt.

Iacobus Madison Condiciōnēs relinquere et novam constitūtiōnem

scrībere voluit. Multōs librōs dē antīquīs cīvitātibus et rēbus

pūblicīs eōrum legēbat. Litterās Polybiī, Graecī Historicī, lēgit.

Polybius dē magnā Rōmānā Rē Pūblicā scripsit. Eam esse optimam

dēclārāvit, quod et duōs consulēs et sēnātum dēlectōs ā populīs

habuit. Rītū illius reī pūblicae, Iacobus consilium Virginiae creāvit.

Constitūtiō Cīvitātium Americae Foederātārum

Id ūnum Praesidentem, Sēnātum, et Domum Lēgātōrum habet.

Populī omnēs hōs magistratūs dēligunt. Consilium etiam fortem

centralem rem pūblicam, quae cīvitātēs regit, confirmat. Virginia

Iacobum cum consiliō ad Conventum Constitūtum mīsit. Eventus

conventūs erat Constitūtiō Cīvitātis Americae Foederātārum.

Iacobus magnam partem huius novae constitūtiōnis scripsit. Hodie,

eum "Patrem Constitūtiōnis" appellāmus.

GLOSSARY & NOTES:

Cīvitātēs Americae Foederātae = The United States of America

Condiciōnēs Societātis = The Articles of Confederation

administrō, āre, āvī, ātum, to govern

constitūtiō, constitūtiōnis, f., constitution

voluit = he wanted < perfect tense of volo, velle, volui, to want

rēs pūblica = government (literally, the matter of the people)

litterās, in the plural form this is best translated as 'writings' or 'literature'

Polybius, ī, m., Polybius

> Polybius (c. 200 – 118 B.C.) is one of the most important early historians. He wrote the History of Rome to 146 B.C. James Madison, who was well versed in both Latin and Greek, studied these accounts in the original Greek.

eam esse optimam = it is the best   (literally, it to be the best)

consul, consulis, m. consul, highest office in the Roman Republic

dēlectōs, perfect passive participle = elected, chosen < dēligō, dēligere, dēlēgī, dēlectum

ā populīs, ablative of agent = by the people

rītus, ūs, m., manner, ritual

> ritū + genitive = in the manner of . . .

Consilium Virginae – The Virginia Plan was devised by James Madison and presented by the Virginia Delegation at the Constitutional Convention.

praesidens, praesidentis, m. president

Senātus, ūs, m., the Senate. The word sēnātus is related to senex, old man, and originally referred to a council of elders. Even in America, one has to meet age requirements before running for office: 25 for House of Representatives, 30 for Senate, and 35 for President

legatōrum – best translated here as ' of representatives'

Domus Legatōrum = House of Representatives

dēligō, dēligere, dēlēgī, dēlectum, to elect, choose (cf. dēlectōs above) centralis, adj. central

>centralem rem publicam – This refers to the federalist view of a strong central government which was adopted by the writers of the Constitution.

quae, nom., sing., relative pronoun referring to *rem publicam* – which

Conventum Constitūtum = Constitutional Convention

RESPONDĒ LATĪNĒ:

1. Quid erat prīmam lēgem patriae?

2. Cūr Iacobus Madison novam constitūtiōnem scrībere voluit?

3. Quis est Polybius?

4. Quis magtistratūs Rōmae dēlēgit?

5. Cūr Iacobum "Patrem Constitūtiōnis" appellāmus?

Quid – what?
Cūr – why?
Quis – who?

CAPUT XXVI

Fundentēs Patrēs
MDCCLXXVI - MDCCLXXXVIII A.D.

T he men who came together in order to declare America's Independence, fight for her freedom, and form her government are reverently referred to as her Founding Fathers. Some of these men, such as Benjamin Franklin, George Washington, Thomas Jefferson, and James Madison are well-known. But there are others worthy to claim that title who are not so well remembered. They too signed the Declaration of Independence and witnessed the birth pangs of America.

GORGIUS WYTHE

Gorgius erat magister lēgis. Multī patrum nostrae patriae erant

discipulī eius, etiam Thoma Jeffersonius et Iacobus Madison.

Thoma eum "patrem secundum" appellāvit. Erat absēns cum

virī Dēclārātiōnem Lībertātis obsignāverant, sed locum maximae significātiōnis eī in illā litterā servāvērunt. Nam hic erat

honestissimus vir omnium.

THOMA NELSON

Imperātor Thoma Nelson Eboracī Oppidī erat vir maximārum

dīvitiārum. Trēs milia copiārum, sub imperium Vasingtoniī, in

bellō Eboracī Oppidī duxit. Britannicī mīlitēs intrō domum eius

cōnfūgerant. Familia eius quamquam intrō domum nōn erant,

Americanī iaculārī negāvērunt. "Cūr meam domum servātis?" eōs

rogavit. Mīlitēs respondērunt, "propter respectum tibi." "Dāte mihi hoc tormentum!" clāmāvit. Statim hic imperātor domum

suam tormentō verberāvit.

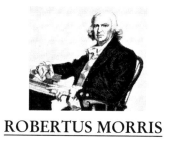

ROBERTUS MORRIS

Robertus Morris erat "Argentārius Rebelliōnis." Congressiō hunc

"Cūrātōrem Fiscī" fēcit. Aliōs mūtuam pecūniam dāre rogāvit;

prīmam argentariam tabernam prosperam patriae creāvit; et suam

fortūnam etiam commeatuī et salāriīs mīlitum dedit. Post bellum hic

vir, sine quō America vincere nōn potuit, ad vincula dēbitōrum īvit.

Fundentēs Patrēs

IACOBUS WILSON

Hic vir Iacobum Madison Constitūtiōnem scrībere adiuvāvit. Hic

et Robertus Morris sunt duo ex paucīs virīs quī et Dēclārātiōnem

Lībertātis et Constitūtiōnem obsignāvērunt. Praesidens

Vasingtonius Iacobum iūdicem in prīmō Iūdiciō Suprēmō fēcit.

CARTER BRAXTON

Carter consilium victōriae habuit. Servōs conscrībere voluit. Sī

servī prō Americā pugnābit, lībertī erunt. Prīmō magistratūs

Fundentēs Patrēs

consilium negāvērunt. Dēnique, autem, quinque mīlia Aethiopēs

erant mīlitēs Americanī. Carter etiam commeātūs exercituī dedit.

Fundentēs Patrēs

GLOSSARY & NOTES:

Gorgius Wythe, m., George Wythe

> George Wythe was a highly regarded lawyer and teacher. Many of the delegates who signed the Declaration of Independence and the Constitution had been his pupils. He was the most highly esteemed man among those serving on the Continental Congress.

etiam, adv., even

cum, adv., when

obsignō, āre, āvī, ātum, to sign

significātiō, significātiōnis, f., significance

honestissimus, a, um, superlative adj., most honest

Thoma Nelson, m., Thomas Nelson

> Thomas Nelson was a signer of the Declaration of Independence who was made general of Virginia's troops. He contributed three million dollars out of his own pocket to prepare for the Battle of Yorktown. He lost his fortune in support of liberty. He was later sent to debtors' prison when he could no longer pay his debts.

cōnfugiō, cōnfugere, cōnfūgī, to take refuge

intrō, prep. + acc., inside

iacularī = to shoot at < iaculor, iacularī, iaculatus sum, deponent verb

verberō, verberāre, verberāvī, verberātum, to beat

tormentō verberāre = to bombard (literally, to beat with the cannon)

> General Nelson ordered the destruction of his own house and property in order to defeat the British at Yorktown. Although once a tremendously wealthy man, he died in poverty.

Robertus Morris, m., Robert Morris

> It was Robert Morris who found the blankets, tents, clothing, and other supplies given to the troops suffering during the winter at Valley Forge. It has been said that independence could not have been won without him.

argentārius, ī, m., financier

rebelliō, rebelliōnis, f., revolution, rebellion

Fundentēs Patrēs

cūrātor, cūrātōris, m., superintendent

fiscus, ī, m., finance

mūtuam pecūniam dāre = to loan (literally, to give borrowed money)

argentaria taberna, f., bank (literally, money shop)

prosperus, a, um, adj., successful

salārium, ī, n., pay; the official regular pay to persons of a military post

> salārium is derived from another Latin word sal (salt). The Roman army used to pay soldiers with salt instead of coins. Salt was a prized mineral that could be bartered for goods. From this word we derive "salary."

quō, ablative, sing., m., relative pronoun, whom

vinculum, ī, n., chain; n.pl. prison

> vincula dēbitōrum = debtors' prison

Iacobus Wilson, m., James Wilson

> Only James Madison contributed more to the writing of the Constitution than James Wilson. Like Robert Morris, James Wilson also spent much of his fortune in supporting the pursuit of liberty. They accrued many debts that they were unable to pay, and thus spent several years in debtors' prison after the war.

quī, nom., sing., m., relative pronoun, who

iūdicium, ī, n., court

suprēmus, a, um, adj., highest, supreme

Carter Braxton, m. Carter Braxton

> Carter Braxton was a legislator of Virginia who proposed recruiting slaves to fight in the colonial militias. In return for military service, slaves would be granted freedom. This recruitment strategy had already worked well for the British military. Many colonists had lost their slaves to the army of their enemy.

conscrībō, conscrībere, conscripsī, conscriptum, to enlist, recruit (for military service)

prīmō = at first

Fundentēs Patrēs

RESPONDĒ LATĪNĒ:

1. Cūr Thoma domum tormentō verberāvit?

2. Cūr Robertum "Argentārum Rebellionis" appellāmus?

3. Quid officium Praesidens Vasingtonius Iacobō dedit?

4. Quōs Gorgius docuit?

5. Quōs Carter conscrībere voluit?

Cūr – why?
Quid – what?
Quōs - whom?

CAPUT XXVII

Prīmus Praesidens
MDCCLXXXIX - MDCCXCVII
A.D.

Sextō decimō diē Aprilis, Gorgius Vasingtonius domum

in Virginiā relīquit. Collēgium Ēlectōrum consensū omnium

eum prīmum Praesidentem Cīvitātium Americae Foederātātum

dēlēgerat. Vasingtonius erat anxius, "Possumne hanc patriam

novam lībertātis bene regere?" Sē dubitāvit. In suō praediō manēre

cupīvit. Tamen, patria eum appellāverat, et eam nōn negāvit.

Novum Eboracum prōcessit. Secundum viam populī

multōrum oppidōrum clāmāvērunt et illō plausērunt. Novum

Prīmus Praesidens

Eboracum Urbem advenit, et in Foderātum Conciliābulum

ascendit. In podiō illī aedificiī ante magnam turbam cīvium,

Gorgius Vasingtonius in officium Praesidentis Cīvitātium Americae

Foederātārum iūrāvit.

Vasingtonius octōs annōs patriae bene servīvit. Dēnique

Vasingtonius, laetus esse cīvis, domum revertit. Cum ille vir

optime perīvit, tōta patria lūxit. In Europā, Britannica classis et

exercitus Napoleonis eum laudāvērunt. Gorgius Vasingtonius,

prīmus Praesidens, erat, "prīmus in bellō, prīmus in pace, et prīmus

in cordibus cīvium."

Prīmus Praesidens

GLOSSARY & NOTES:

sextō decimō diē, ablative of time when

Collēgium Ēlectōrum, n. Electoral College (literally, College of Electors)

consensus, ūs, m. consensus

consensū omnium = unamimously (literally, by the consent of all)

sē, acc., sing., m. himself

plaudō, plaudere, plausī, plausum, (+dative) to applaud

Novum Eboracum Urbem, accusative of place where

The names of towns and cities do not use a Latin preposition with expressions of place (i.e. place from which, to which, and place where).

Foederātum Conciliābulum, n. Federal Hall

Washington D.C. was not the original capitol of the United States, indeed that district did not even exist yet. Washington was sworn in at Federal Hall, located on Wall Street in New York City.

podium, ī, n. balcony

in officium . . . iūrāvit = he swore to observe the office . . .

The Romans used the verb iūrāre (to swear, take an oath) with in + accusative to convey this idea. Literally, he is "swearing into" an office. This is similar to our phrase the "swearing in" of a public servant.

octō annōs, accusative of duration of time

laetus esse cīvis, Many of the world's leaders, including King George III, were amazed that a man holding such power, could lay it down of his own free will and return to the life of an ordinary citizen.

domum = to home, homeward

Like the names of towns and cities, the noun *domus* does not use a Latin preposition with expressions of place.

vir optimē = best man

This phrase was used by the Romans as a sign of respect, such as we use "mister" or "sir". It was used particularly for men of great authority and position.

Prīmus Praesidens

Napoleon, Napoleonis, m. Napoleon Bonaparte

eum laudāvērunt, best translated = paid him tribute

"prīmus . . . cīvium eius.", These are the famous words of Henry Lee, Revolutionary War Hero, Virginia Congressman, and father of Robert E. Lee, upon the death of Washington.

RESPONDĒ LATĪNĒ:

1. Quis praesidentem dēlēgit?

2. Cūr erat Vasingtonius anxius?

3. Ubī Vasingtonius in officium iūrāvit?

4. Quot annī erat praesidens?

5. Quis mortem Vasingtoniī lūxit?

CAPUT XXVIII

Emptiō Louisianae
MDCCCIII A.D.

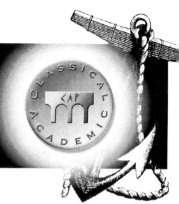

Thoma Jeffersonius erat tertius Praesidens Cīvitātium

Americae Foederātārum. Haec administrātiō est nōta propter

Emptiōnem Louisianae. Gallicus explōrātor, Rene Cavelier de La

Salle, hanc terram prō Galliā invēnerat. Gallicī Novam Aureliam

in Louisianā funderant. Haec colōnia erat ad ōstium magnī

Flūminis Mississippiēnsis. America hōc flūmine mercatūrae eguit.

Nam mercatūra terrā erat tarda, sed mercatūra aquā erat celeris.

Napoleon, dux Galliae, autem novum imperium occidentale condere

Emptiō Louisianae

cupīvit. Americanōs Flūmine Mississippiēnsis utī nōn voluit.

Praesidens erat sollicitus. Et Novam Aureliam et auctōritātem

flūminis emere necesse erat.

Ita Praesidens Jeffersonius Robertum Livingston ad

Galliam mīsit. Napoleon diū agere nōn voluit. Deinde Praesidens

Jeffersonius Iacobum Monroe mīsit, quī antehāc ē Galliā expulsus

erat. Adventus eius erat gravis. Subito, Napoleon suam mentem

mūtāvit. Pecūniā bellō in Europā eguit. Nōn modo Novam

Aureliam, sed etiam tōtam Louisianam Americae vēndidit.

Emptiō Louisianae

GLOSSARY & NOTES:

administrātiō, administrātiōnis, f. administration

emptiō, emptiōnis, f. purchase

Rene Cavelier de La Salle, French explorer who discovered the mouth of the Mississippi River on April 6, 1682, and claimed the surrounding lands for France.

Nova Aurelia, f. New Orleans

ōstium, -ī, n. mouth (of a river)

Mississippiēnsis, e, adj. of Mississippi

egeō, egēre, eguī, (+ abl.) to need (literally, to have need for...)

occidentalis, e, adj. west

ūtī (+ abl.) = to use < ūtor, ūtī, deponent verb

voluit = he did not want < volō, velle, voluī

Robertus Livingston, m. Robert Livingston

> Robert Livingston was appointed the resident minister at the court of Napoleon in 1801 by President Jefferson. He negotiated the purchase of the Louisiana Territory.

agere, best translated here as "to negotiate"

Iacobus Monroe, m. James Monroe

> President Jefferson appointed James Monroe as resident extraordinary and asked him to help Robert Livingston with the negotiations in France. James Monroe later served two terms as the fifth President of the United States (1817 – 1825).

quī, nom. sing. relative pronoun, who

antehāc, adv., before this time, earlier

expulsus erat, perfect passive, he had been expelled < expellō, expellere, expulī, expulsus

> James Madison had been temporarily expelled from France during his last mission to that country.

Emptiō Louisianae

nōn modo . . . sed etiam = not only . . . but also
vēndō, vēndere, vēndidī, vēnditum, to sell

RESPONDĒ LATĪNĒ:

1. Quis Louisianam invēnerat?

2. Cūr America magnō flūmine eguit?

3. Quem Praesidens ad Galliam mīsit?

4. Quās terrās Gallia Americae vēndidit?

Quis – who (sing.)
Cūr – why?
Quī – who (pl.)
Quās – which?

THE
LOUISIANA
PURCHASE (1803)

MILES
100 50 0   100   200   300

CAPUT XXIX

Lewis et Clark
MDCCCV A.D.

Mandātō Praesidentis Jeffersoniī, Lewis et Clark immēnsem

terram novam Emptiōnis Louisianae explōrāvērunt. Iter propter

multās sententiās fēcērunt. Caput Flūminis Mississippiēnsis,

consuētūdinēs indigenārum, et geōgraphiam terrae quondam

incognitae invenīre voluērunt. Sacajawea, indigena fēmina,

explōratōrēs in colloquiō cum aliīs gentibus indigenārum adiuvāvit.

Annō MDCCCV, Lewis et Clark Mare Pacificum attegērunt et

mōx in Sanctum Lewis rediērunt. Quamquam per multa perīcula

Lewis et Clark

iter longum fēcērunt, tamen incolumēs rediērunt.

Narratiōnēs eōrum dē itinere populum tenuērunt. Mōx

aliī fortēs in Territoriam Septentrio-Occidentalem colōniam

dēdūxērunt. Propter iter explōratōrum, Foederatum Cīvitātum

Americae hanc terram patriae nostrae addidit.

Lewis et Clark

GLOSSARY & NOTES:

mandātum, ī, n., an order, instruction, commission, charge;

  mandātō, abl. = by the command

  This is word is from the fourth principal part of *mandō*, taught in Primer B, chapter 9. The ablative is *of the cause*, and it is used to indicate the motive of an agent, and not the object of his action. Properly, we should use *propter* to indicate the object, and not the motive, of an agent, but the usages were confused even in the classical period (AG 404b).

immēnsus, a, um, adj. immeasurable, immense, boundless, vast

facere iter, classical idiom = to make a journey

voluērunt, perf., act., ind., 3ʳᵈ pl., *they wished.* < *volō, velle, voluī*, to wish, want. This verb takes an infinitive, "wish *to____*."

caput, capitis, n., head; origin, source, spring (of a river)

consuētūdo, inis, f., a custom, habit, usage

quondam, adv., formerly, once

incognitus, a, um, adj., unknown

attingō, attingere, atigi, atactum, to approach, arrive at

  ad + tangō = attingō. This word, in its use above, is especially common in classical historians (e.g., Caesar), see entry in *L&S*.

quamquam...tamen = although...nevertheless

narratio, ōnis, f., an account, telling. (compare to *narrō)*

teneo, tenēre, tenuī, tentum, to hold; here, to hold the interest of, captivate

Territoria Septentrio-Occidentalis = Northwest Territory

addō, addere, addidī, additum, (+ dative) to add, to join

Lewis et Clark

RESPONDĒ LATĪNĒ:

1. Cūr Lewis et Clark iter fēcērunt?

2. Quis eōs adiuvāvit?

3. Quōmodo eōs adiuvāvit?

Cūr – why?
Quis – who?
Quōmodo – how, in what manner?
Quot – how many?

CAPUT XXX

Altera Renovatiō
c. MLCCC A.D.

Per bellum Thoma Paine scipserat, "haec sunt tempora

quae animōs hominum probant." Annī bellī nec modo animōs

sed etiam spiritūs hominum probāverant. Gallicī mīlitēs, quī

auxilium Americanīs copiīs tulerant, etiam Ratiōnem Gallicam

tulerant. Haec ratiō Deum ignorāvit et hominem laudāvit.

Multī Americanī id quod crēdiderant dubitābant: "Quis est

vērus Deus? Estne praesēns in vītīs nostrīs? Suntne scriptūrae

vērae?"

Altera Renovatiō

Deus autem populōs nōn relīquit, sed alteram

renovatiōnem tulit. In scholā coepit. Timotheus Dwight

praesidens huius scholae annō MDCCXCIV factus est. Eō

tempore nullī discipulī erant sociī ecclēsiae, sed aperte

scriptūrās dubitāvērunt. Seniōrēs discipulī magistrum et

praesidentem in disputātiōnem prōvocāvērunt. Timotheus

audīvit dum quisque discipulus contrā veritātem scriptūrae

disputāvit. Tandem Magister Timotheus dīxit. Omnem

disputātiōnem dialecticē refellit, deinde scriptūram esse vērum

verbum Deī dēmōnstrāvit. Hic septem annōs dē veritāte verbī

Altera Renovatiō

Deī adnūntiāre persevērāvit. Tandem renovatiō ērūpit et

tertium discipulōrum conversum est. Altera renovatiō magna

et conversiō Novae Angliae incēperant.

Altera Renovatiō

GLOSSARY & NOTES:

renovatiō, renovatiōnis, f., revival

per, best translated here "during"

Thoma Paine, m., Thomas Paine

>Thomas Paine, author of Common Sense and a devout patriot, was also a proponent of the French Rationalist Movement.

nec modo . . . sed etiam = not only . . . but also

Ratio Gallica, f., French Rationalism

>The theory that reason alone, apart from God and spiritual revelation, can arrive at basic truth regarding the world.

ignorō, āre, āvī, ātum, to ignore, disregard

Timotheus Dwight, m., Timothy Dwight

>Timothy Dwight was a grandson of Jonathan Edwards, notable figure of the First Great Awakening. Dwight served as a chaplain in the American militia during the Revolutionary War and became friends with General Washington. In addition to his impressive tenure as President of Yale College, Dwight played an instrumental role in the founding of Andover Seminary.

scholae, The school referred to in this story is Yale University.

factus est = perfect passive tense, he was made < facio, facere, fēcī, factum

eō tempore = at that time

sociī, best translated here "members"

aperte, adv., openly

senior, seniōris, comparative adj., senior, elder

magistrum et praesidentem, At this time in the history of the university the president was required to teach the senior class. In addition to these roles Timothy Dwight also served as Master of Divinity.

disputātiō, diputātiōnis, f., debate

>At this time debates were a required component of the senior class studies.

prōvocō, āre, āvī, ātum, to challenge

Altera Renovatiō

quisque, adj., each, every

disputō, āre, āvī, ātum, to dispute, argue

dialecticē, adv., logically

refellō, refellere, refellī, to refute, prove false

septem annōs, accusative of duration of time = for seven years

adnūntiō, āre, āvī, ātum, to preach (ad + nūntiāre)

persevērō, āre, āvī, ātum, to persist, persevere in

ērumpō, ērumpere, ērūpī, ēruptum, to break out

coversum est, perfect passive, it is converted < convertō, convertere, convertī, conversum

conversiō, conversiōnis, f., conversion (cf. convertō above)

incipiō, incipere, incēpī, inceptum, to begin

RESPONDĒ LATĪNĒ:

1. Cūr Ratiō Gallica erat perīculum?

2. Quis erat Timotheus?

3. Quid discipulī diputāvērunt?

4. Quōmodo magister eōs refellit?

5. Quot annī Timotheus persevērit ante renovatiō ērūpit?

Cūr - why?
Quis - who?
Quid - what?
Quōmodo - in what manner, how?
Quot - how many?

"Old First" erected 1819

CAPUT XXXI

Bellum Annō MDCCCXII
MDCCCXII A.D.

Post Bellum prō Lībertāte Americanā, Foederātum Cīvitātum

Americae et Britannia nōn sociī erant. Bellum annō MDCCCXII

ex duōbus gravibus causīs exstitit. Britannia cum Gallīs bellum

gerēbat. Quod Brittania copiīs eguit, Americanōs in mīlitiam

compulit. Deinde, nāvēs Brittanicae mercātūrae cum aliīs gentibus

Americanae obstitērunt.

Hoc contrā Britanniam bellum ā Bellō prō Lībertāte Americanā

distulit. In priore bellō, exercitūs in terrā pugnāvērunt; in hōc,

141

nāvēs pugnās gravēs in marī pugnāvērunt. Nova classis Americana

veterī classī Britannicae aemula esse potuit.

Annō MDCCCIV, exercitus Britannicus Vasingtoniam

oppugnāvit. Cūriam Senatūs, Domum Albam, aedificia lēgum,

et domūs accendit. Vasingtoniā, exercitus Britannicus sub

Baltimoriam successit. Ibi, copiae Americanae Britannicōs vīcērunt.

Hodiē, Americanī hoc bellum commemorant quod Franciscus Scott

Key carmen patriae nostrae dē proeliō Baltimoriae scripsit.

Bellum Annō MDCCCXII

GLOSSARY & NOTES:

exsistō, stāre, stitī, stitum, to proceed, arise, issue from (derivative of *stāre*)

bellum gerere, classical idiom = to wage war

mīlitia, ae, f., military service, the military. Which other Latin words does this remind you of?

compellō, compellere, compulī, compulsum, to force, impel, compel

in, prep. + acc., into, against (here)

obstō, obstāre, obstitī, obstātūrus, (+dative) to stand before; to hinder, prevent (*ob* + *stō)*

differō, differre, distulī, dīlātum, to differ; with ā/ab + ablative = be different (from)

prior, ius, comparative adj., prior, former, earlier (compare to *prīmus*)

aemulus, a, um, adj., a rival (to), competitive (with), takes a dative of person/thing rivaled

Vasingtonia, ae, f., Washington, D.C

> Vasingtoniā, ablative of place from which. For the names of cities the ablative without a preposition is used to express motion away from.

Cūria, ae, f., a building where the Senate (of Rome) held its sessions

> Here, *curia senatus* refers to the capitol building, where the congress meets.

accendō, accendere, acendī, acensus, to set afire, to kindle.

succēdō, succedere, successī, successum, to come up under; (here, and in military contexts) to march on, advance, approach

carmen, carminis, n. song, poem

Baltimoria, ae, f., Baltimore, Maryland

Bellum Annō MDCCCXII

RESPONDĒ LATĪNĒ:

1. Quid est causa bellī annō MDCCCXII?

2. Quandō Britannicus Vasingtoniam oppugnāvit?

3. Quid Britannicus in Vasingtoniā fēcērunt?

4. Quid Franciscus Scott Key scripsit?

Quid - what?
Quandō – where?
Quid – what?

CAPUT XXXII

Comprōmissum dē Missuriā

MDCCCXX A.D.

Terra Louisianae in variās regiōnēs dīvīsa est. Ūna ē

regiōnibus erat Missuria. Populī Missuriae, quī duo mīlia servōs

habuērunt, cīvitātēm esse cupivērunt. Lēgātus Novī Eboracī hanc

cīvitātem novam esse lībertam cupivit. "Voluntātem meōrum

electōrum sciō, " dēclārāvit, "et incūriōsus consequentiārum, eam

affirmābō; Ego, lēgātus eōrum, ōdium eōrum servitūtī in omne

formā dēclārābō." Haec prōpositiō in Domō Legatōrum vicit,

in quā lībertae cīvitātēs maiorem partem habuērunt. In Sēnātū

145

Comprōmissum dē Missuriā

autem prōpositiō nōn vicit. Nam numerus lībertārum cīvitātum et

cīvitātum quae servitūtem sustinuērunt erat aequus.

Diū erat magna contrōversia. Utraque factiō potestātem

alterius timuit. Dēnique comprōmissum facere potuērunt.

Cenomannica, quae erat pars Massaciusettae, lībertam cīvitātem

suam esse cupivit. Simul et Cenomannica et Missuria cīvitātēs

factae sunt. Lex servitūtem in primō prohibuit, sed nōn in secundō.

Lex etiam servitūtem in terrā quae erat septemtriōnālis ab australe

fīnem Missuriae prohibuit. Illa pars lēgis autem brevī tempore

modo remansit. Iterum et iterum novae cīvitātēs lībram potestātis

Comprōmissum dē Missuriā

impenduērunt, quae Americam sēcum bellum gerere dūxit.

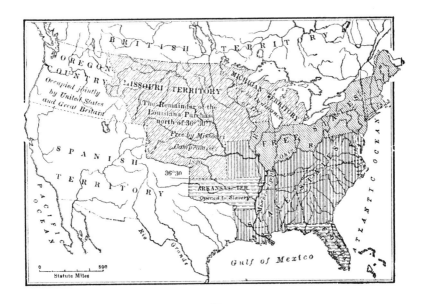

Comprōmissum dē Missuriā

GLOSSARY & NOTES:

comprōmissum, ī, n., compromise

> In antiquity this word literally was defined as a mutual agreement to abide by an arbiter's decision. From this idea we derived the word "compromise".

Missuria, ae, f., Missouri

dīvīsa est, perfect passive = it was divided < dīvidō, dīvidere, dīvīsī, dīvīsum

regiō, regiōnis, f., territory, region

lēgātus, ī, m., representative

> In February 1819, New York Representative James Tallmadge put forth a proposition to ban slavery in Missouri as a condition for statehood even though there were more than 2,000 slaves already living there.

incūriōsus, a, um, adj., regardless, unconcerned, indifferent

consequentia, ae, f., consequence, natural outcome

odium, ī, n., hatred, dislike

servitūs, servitūtis, f., slavery

prōpositiō, prōpositiōnis, f., proposition

maior, maioris, comparative adj., greater

> maior pars = majority (literally, greater part)

sustineō, sustinēre, sustinuī, sustentum, to uphold, support

contrōversia, ae, f., controversy

uterque, utraque, utrumque, adj., each (of the two)

factiō, factiōnis, f., party, faction

alterius, gen. sing. form of alter

> *alter* is one of the special –ius adjectives. These appear to be normal 1st & 2nd declension adjectives in all cases except the genitive and dative singular. In these two forms they have

Comprōmissum dē Missuriā

endings like those of *ille*.

Cenomannica, ae, f., Maine

Massaciusetta, ae, f., Massachusettes

factae sunt, perfect passive = they were made, they became

remaneō, remanēre, remansī, remānsum, to remain, continue (re+manēre)

brevī tempore, classical idiom = for a short time

impendeō, impendēre, impenduī, to threaten

lībra, ae, f., balance

sēcum = sē+cum, with itself, herself

Comprōmissum dē Missuriā

RESPONDĒ LATĪNĒ:

1. Cūr Missuria lībertam cīvitātem esse nōn cupivit?

2. Cūr aliī Missuriam lībertam cīvitātem esse cupivērunt?

3. Quae cīvitātēs erant partēs comprōmissī?

4. Ubī comprōmissum servitūtem prohibuit?

5. Quis cum Americā bellum gesserit?

Cūr – why?
Quae – which?
Ubī – where?
Quis – who?

Appendix A

Pledge of Allegiance

Fidem meum obligō vexillō

Cīvitatium Americae Foederātārum

Et reī pūblicae prō quā stat,

Ūnī nātiōne Deō dūcente

Nōn dīvidendae cum lībertāte iūstitiāque omnibus.

GLOSSARY:

dūcente, abl. sing. participle, leading < dūcō, dūcere, dūxī, ductum

dīvidendae = divided < dīvidō, dīvidere, dīvīsī, dīvīsum

Appendix B

Star-Spangled Banner

This song was originally written by Francis Scott Key as a poem entitled "Denfense of Fort McHenry." The poem was inspired by the American victory witnessed by Mr. Key at the Battle of Baltimore during the War of 1812. The poem was later set to music previously composed by a Mr. Smith. The inspiring words moved Americans who immediately adopted the song as an unofficial national anthem. But it was not until March 3, 1931 that the American Congress officially proclaimed it as the national anthem, 116 years after it was first written.

Potestne cernī prīmō diluculō

Vexillum quod vesperī salūtābāmus,

Dum stellās clāvōsque et in proeliō

Fluitantēs superbe in vallō spectāmus?

Atque salvum adhuc interdum subitae

Star-Spangled Banner

Vexillum noctū ostendēbant flammae;

O dic num dēspectet stellans vexillum

Līberam patriam fortiumque domum.

Per vaporēs maris unde instant hostēs

In lītore iam aliquid vix apparet,

Quod aura incūnstāns per celsās turrēs

Modo condit umbra, modo languidē movet;

Ecce tandem prīmī sōlis sub lūmen

Clārō splendet colōre vexillī aqua;

Star-Spangled Banner

Atque diū dēspectet stellans vexillum

Līberam patriam fortiumque domum.

Ō semper sic fiat cum suās domōs

Ab exitiō populōs līber dēfendet;

Quodque nūmen tuetur arās et focōs

Dīvīnitus victrix rēs pūblica laudet.

Superant semper iūstum quī causam habent

Et in Deō spem pōnere omnem solent;

Sic triumphans dēspectet stellans vexillum

Līberam patriam fortiumque domum.

Star-Spangled Banner

GLOSSARY & NOTES:

<u>fluitantēs,</u> acc. pl. participle, streaming < fluō, fluere, fluxī, fluxum

<u>stellans,</u> nom. sing. participle, star-spangled

> (participles should be treated as adjectives)

<u>despectet,</u> subjunctive present = may it look down upon

> The subjunctive mood is often used for expressions of hope or wishes.

<u>incōnstāns, incōnstantis,</u> adj., inconsistent, fickle, shaky

<u>modo . . . modo</u> = now . . . now, at one moment . . . at another

<u>fiat,</u> 3rd person sing., present subjunctive = may it be

<u>tuetur,</u> 3rd sing, pres, he defends < tueor, tuērī, tuitus sum, deponent verb

<u>laudet,</u> subjunctive present = may he praise

<u>triumphans,</u> nom, sing. participle, triumphing

Bibliographia

GRAMMAR REFERENCES & LEXICA

Allen and Greenough. New Latin Grammar. New Rochelle, NY: Caratzas, Aristiede D., 1992.

Crane, Gregory R. (ed.) The Perseus Project, *http://www.perseus.tufts.edu*, *July 2004*

Lewis and Short. A Latin Dictionary. Oxford: Clarendon Press, 1879.

Glare, et alii. Oxford Latin Dictionary. Oxford: Clarendon Press, 1982.

Wheelock, Frederic M. Wheelock's Latin, 6th edition. New York, NY: HaperCollins, 2000.

HISTORICAL REFERENCES

"An Account of Magellan by Ortelius"
URL: http://www.orteliusmaps.com/book/ort_text12.html

"Black Man Slays Officer that Attempted to Seize Gun." Public Intelligence Review and Newsletter, Volume 1, Nr. 7. August 10, 1994.

Bibliographia

Callander, Guy Stevens (ed). Selections from the Economic History of the United States. Boston: Ginn and Co., 1909

Kalm, Peter. "Travels into North America." 1749.

Drucker-Hunsaker, Susan, Darlene Conwell, and Jose Manuel Ochoa. "The American Revolution"
URL: http://www.usfca.edu/fac-staff/conwell/revolution/openingpage.htm

"Explorers to 1815 History Series." Veritas Press, 2001.

Fox, Stephen. "Timothy Dwight." November, 1995.
URL: http://dylee.keel.econ.ship.edu/ubf/leaders/dwight.htm

Fradin, Dennis Brindell. The Signers: The 56 Stories Behind the Declaration of Independence. New York: Walker & Company, 2002.

Fradin, Dennis Brindell. The Thirteen Colonies. Chicago: Children's Press, c.1988.

Grant, Matthew G. Champlain, Explorer of New France. Mankato, MN: Creative Education, 1974.

Meltzer, Milton (ed). The American Revolutionaries: A History in Their Own Words 1750 – 1800. New York: Thomas Crowell Junior Books.

Morris, Richard B. and James Woodress (ed). Voices From America's Past, Vol.1. New York: E.P. Dutton & Co.

Murray, Iain H. Jonathan Edwards, A New Biography. Pennsylvania: The Banner of Truth Trust, 1996.

Prescott's Conquest of Mexico, University of Virginia hypertext,
URL: http://xroads.virginia.edu/ ~ HYPER/PRESCOTT/bk02_ch01.html, July 2004.

Bibliographia

Pushee, George D. III. "Joseph Warren, Martyr of Bunker Hill." April 7, 1994.
URL: http://members.aol.com/VAYORKRT/AMDJWP.html

"Sancti Ephiphanii ad Physiologum." Ponce de Leon.
URL: http://gateway.uvic.ca/spcoll/physiologum/index.html.

"Spanish Colony 1565 – 1898"
URL: http://www.ualberta.ca/ ~ vmitchel/fw2.html.

Stein, R. Conrad. Cornerstones of Freedom: The Story of Valley Forge. Regensteiner Publishing Enterprises Inc., 1985

The New Encylopaedia Britannica, 15th ed. Encyclopaedia Britannica Inc.

Glossary

a, ab (1)	prep. + abl. from, away from, by
absēns, absentis (6)	adj. absent
accēdō, accēdere, accessī, accessum (1)	3, to reach, get to, approach
accendō, accendere, acendī, acensus (31)	3, to set afire, to kindle
acerbus, a, um (9)	adj. harsh, bitter, painful
ad (2)	prep. + acc. to, toward, near, at
addō, addere, addidī, additum (29)	3, (+dat.) to add
adiuvō, āre, āvī, ātum (9)	1, to help, give aide
administrātiō, administrātiōnis (28)	f. administration
administrō, āre, āvī, ātum (25)	1, to govern, manage
adoptō, āre, āvī, ātum (25)	1, to adopt
adsum, adesse, adfuī, adfutūrum (20)	irreg. to be present
adulēscēns, adulēscentis (5)	m/f. youth, young person
adulescentia, ae (4)	f. youth
adveniō, advenīre, advēnī, adventum (6)	4, to arrive
adventus, ūs (20)	m. arrival
aedificium, ī (27)	n. building
aedificō, āre, āvī, ātum (8)	1, to build
aedituus, ī (19)	m. sexton (church attendant)

Glossary

aeger, aegra, aegrum (7)	adj. sick
aemulus, a, um (31)	adj. a rival (to), competitive (with); takes a dative of person/thing rivaled
aequus, a, um (32)	adj. equal
aerārium, ī (2)	n. treasury
Aethiops, Aethiopis (24)	m. Ethiopian, black person
affirmō, āre, āvī, ātum (18)	1, to affirm, assert
Africa, ae (1)	f. Africa
ager, agrī (13)	m. field
agō, agere, egī, actum (8)	3, to do, drive, discuss; negotiate
agricola, ae (7)	m. farmer
albus, a, um (6)	adj. white (used as surname for John White, ch.6)
alius, alia, aliud (3)	adj. other, another
alter, altra, altrum (32)	adj. other (of two)
altus, a, um (14)	adj. high
amātus, a, um (20)	adj. beloved < amatum - supine of amāre
America, ae (4)	f. America
Americanus, a, um ()	adj. American
amīca, ae (20)	f. female friend
amīcus, ī (5)	m. friend
amō, āre, āvī, ātum (7)	1, to love
amoenus, a, um (4)	adj. pleasant (esp. of places)
Anglia, ae (10)	f. England
Anglicus, a, um (10)	adj. English
animal, animalis (13)	n. animal
Anna, ae (11)	f. Anne
annus, ī (1)	m. year
ante (3)	prep. + acc. before; adv. before
antehāc (28)	adv. before this time, earlier
antīquus, a, um (19)	adj. old, ancient

Glossary

anxius, a, um (27)	adj. anxious
apellātiō, apellātiōnis (2)	f. title
aperiō, aperīre, aperuī, apertum (16)	4, to uncover, reveal
apertus, a, um (23)	adj. open
appellō, āre, āvī, ātum (3)	1, to call, name
April, Aprilis (27)	f. April
aptus, a, um (1)	adj. fitted for, stuited for (used with 'ad' + accusative)
apud (20)	prep. + acc. with, among
aqua, ae (28)	f. water
Arabicus, a, um (24)	adj. Arabian
arbor, arboris (13)	f. tree
argentāria, ae (26)	f. bank
argentārius, ī (26)	m. financier
arō, āre, āvī, ātum (13)	1, to plow
ascendō, ascendere, ascendī, ascēnsum (13)	3, to climb
Asia, ae (1)	f. Asia
astrologia, ae (1)	f. astronomy, the study of the stars
attingō, attingere, attigī, attactum (29)	3, to touch, come in contact with; approach, arrive
auctoritās, auctoritātis (28)	f. authority, power
audāx, audācis (5)	adj. bold, daring
audiō, audīre, audīvī, audītum (14)	4, to listen, hear
Augustus, ī (8)	m. August (month)
aurum, ī (7)	n. gold
australis, e (15)	adj. southern
aut (13)	conj. or
autem (7)	conj. however
autumnus, ī (9)	m. autumn

Glossary

auxilium, ī (7)	n. aide, help
āvehō, āvehere, āvexī, āvectum (12)	3, to carry away; (pass.) to ride away
Aztecus, ī (4)	m. Aztec, native inhabitant of Mexico
baculum, ī (12)	n. stick
Baltimoria, ae (31)	f. Baltimore
bene (9)	adv. well
beneficium, ī (22)	n. benefit
Biblia, ōrum (13)	n.pl. The Bible
bibō, bibere, bibī (20)	3, to drink
bis (8)	adv. twice
bonus, a, um (5)	adj. good
Bostonia, ae (10)	f. Boston
Bostoniēnsis, e (10)	adj. of Boston
brevis, breve (7)	adj. short, brief
Britannia, ae (6)	f. Britain, England
Britannicī, ōrum (16)	m. British (people)
Brittanicus, a, um (16)	adj. British
butyrum, ī (15)	n. butter
cadō, cadere, cecidī, cāsum (16)	3, to fall
caedō, caedere, cecīdī, caesum (13)	3, to chop down, cut down, fell
calceus, ī (23)	m. shoe
calidus, a, um (20)	adj. warm, hot
California, ae (4)	f. California
calix, calicis (20)	m. cup
candela, ae (13)	f. candle
canis, canis (12)	m/f. dog
cantō, āre, āvī, ātum (23)	1, to sing
capiō, capere, cēpī, captum (9)	3, to seize, take
captivus, ī (22)	m. prisoner (of war)

Glossary

caput, capitis (12)	n. head; origin, source, spring (of a river)
carbō, carbōnis (17)	m. charcoal
carmen, carminis (31)	n. song
caro, carnis (15)	f. meat
Carolus, ī (3)	m. Charles
carrus, ī (14)	m. wagon, cart
cārus, a, um (13)	adj. dear, expensive, costly
casa, ae (8)	f. house
castellum, ī (16)	n. fort
castor, castoris (23)	m. beaver
castra, ōrum (23)	n.pl. (military) camp
causa, ae (21)	f. cause
celer, celeris, celere (8)	adj. quick, swift
celeriter (16)	adv. quickly
cēnō, āre, āvī, ātum (9)	1, to dine
Cenomannica, ae (32)	f. Maine
centralis, e (25)	adj. central
centum (7)	numerical adj. hundred
cēterus, a, um (4)	adj. the other(s), the remaining, the rest
charta, ae (11)	f. charter
chartographia, -ae (1)	f. cartography, study of map-making
Christoforus, ī (2)	m. Christopher
cibus, ī (23)	m. food
circumnāvigō, āre, āvī, ātum (3)	1, to sail around
cista, ae (17)	f. chest
cīvis, cīvis (17)	m/f. citizen
cīvitās, cīvitātis (4)	f. state, commonwealth
clāmō, āre, āvī, ātum (6)	1, to shout
clāmor, clāmōris (16)	m. shout, cry
clārus, a, um (3)	adj. clear, famous

Glossary

classis, classis (2)	f. fleet (of ships)
claudō, claudere, clausī, clausum (18)	3, to close
clāvis, clāvis (17)	f. key
coffea Arabica (24)	f. coffee
cognōscō, cognōscere, cognōvī, cognitum (22)	3, to become aquainted with, learn
cōgō, cōgere, coēgī, coāctum (12)	3, to force
collegium, ī (27)	n. college, guild (of magistrates)
collis, collis (20)	m. hill
colōnia, -ae (6)	f. colony
colōnus, ī (6)	m. colonist
comes, comitis (3)	m. companian
commeātus, ūs (22)	m. (military) supplies
commūtō, āre, āvī, ātum (13)	1, to trade (with cum + abl.)
compellō, compellere, compulī, compulsum (31)	3, to force, compel
comprōmissum, ī (32)	n. compromise
conciliābulum, ī (27)	n. hall; place for public gatherings
condiciō, condiciōnis (25)	f. term, condition, article
condō, condere, condidī, conditum	3, to build, found, establish
cōnfigō, cōngfigere, cōnfixī, cōnfixum (23)	3, to bind together
cōnfīnium, ī (2)	n. boundary, borderline
confirmō, āre, āvī, ātum (25)	1, to confirm
cōnfugiō, cōnfugere, cōnfūgī (26)	3, to take refuge
congressiō, congressiōnis (18)	f. meeting, conference; congress
cōnscendō, cōnscendere, cōnscendī, cōnscēnsum (17)	3, to board (a ship)
cōnscrībō, cōnscrībere, cōnscripsī, cōnscriptum (26)	3, to enlist, recruit (mil.)
cōnsēnsus, ūs (27)	m. consensus

Glossary

cōnsequentia, ae (32)	f. consequence
cōnsilium, ī (19)	n. plan
consitūtiō, constitūtiōnis (25)	f. constitution
cōnstituō, cōnstituere, cōnstituī, cōnstitūtum (5)	3, to set up, establish
constitūtus, a, um (25)	adj. constitutional
cōnsuētūdō, cōnsuētūdinis (29)	f. custom, habit, usage
consul, consulis (25)	m. consul (highest office of the Roman Republic)
continēns, continentis (18)	adj. continental
contrā (16)	prep. + acc. against
contrōversia, ae (32)	f. controversy
conveniō, convenīre, convēnī, conventum (16)	4, to come together
conventus, ūs (25)	m. meeting, convention
convīvium, ī (9)	n. feast, banquet; party
copia, ae (6)	f. supply, abundance; plural form (military) troops
coquō, coquere, coxī, coctum (13)	3, to cook
cor, cordis (6)	n. heart
corpus, corporis (24)	n. body
Cortesius, ī (4)	m. Cortez
crās (20)	adv. tomorrow
crēdō, crēdere, crēdidī, crēditum (9)	3, (+ dative of person, + accusative of thing) to trust, trust in
creō, āre, āvī, ātum (7)	1, to create
crescō, crescere, crēvī, crētum (18)	3, to increase
crustulum, ī (15)	n. biscuit, cookie
cultūra, ae (9)	f. culture, cultivation
cum (1)	prep. + abl. with; adv. when
cupiō, cupīre, cupīvī, cupītum (16)	4, to desire eagerly
cūr (12)	interrogative adv., why?

Glossary

cūra, ae (21)	f. care
cūrātor, cūrātōris (26)	m. superintendent
Cūria, ae (31)	f. Senate House
cūrō, āre, āvī, ātum (13)	1, to care for
currō, currere, cucurrī, cursum (14)	3, to run
cursus, ūs (21)	m. course
deamon, daemonis (12)	m. devil
dēbeō, dēbēre, debuī, debitum (15)	2, (+ infinitive) to owe, ought, must
dēbitor, dēbitōris (26)	m. debtor
decem (15)	numerical adj. ten
dēclārātiō, dēclārātiōnis (18)	f. declaration
dēcrescō, dēcrescere, dēcrēvī, dēcrētum (18)	3, to diminish, decrease
dēcrētum, ī (18)	n. decree, act
dēdūcō, dēdūcere, dēduxī, dēductum (10)	3, to lead out
dēfendō, dēfendere, dēfendī, dēfensum (20)	3, to defend, protect
dēfessus, a, um (8)	adj. tired
deinde (4)	adv. then
Delawar (22)	m. Delaware River
dēlectus (25)	see dēligō
dēleō, dēlēre, dēlēvī, dēlētum (17)	2, to destroy
dēligō, dēligere, dēlēgī, dēlectum (25)	3, to choose
dēmōnstrō, āre, āvī, ātum (2)	1, to show, point out
dēnique (1)	adv. finally
deorsum (5)	adv. down, downwards
dēprehendō, dēprehendere, dēprehendī, dēprehensum (22)	3, to surprise, to catch off guard
dēspērātus, a, um (22)	adj. desperate, dispirited
dētruncō, āre, āvī, ātum (12)	1, to cut off, behead

Glossary

deus, ī (9)	m. god
dīcō, dīcere, dixī, dictum (12)	3, to speak, say
diēs, diēī (8)	m/f. day
differō, differre, distulī, dīlātum (31)	3, to differ; (with a/ab + abl.) be different from
difficilis, difficile (6)	adj. difficult
dīligens, dīligentis (9)	adj. attentive, careful; diligent
dīligenter (9)	adv. carefully, attentively
dīmittō, dīmittere, dīmīsī, dīmissum (17)	3, to send away
discipulus, ī (10)	m., student
discō, discere, didicī (2)	3, to learn
distans, distantis (5)	adj. distant
dīvidō, dīvidere, dīvīsī, dīvīsum (2)	3, to divide
dīvitiae, ārum (7)	f. pl. riches, wealth
dō, dare, dedī, dātum (1)	1, to give
doceō, docēre, docuī, doctum (9)	2, to teach
doctrīna, ae (1)	f. instruction, teaching, training
dolor, dolōris (23)	f. grief, sorrow, suffering
dominus, ī (2)	m. master, lord
domus, ūs (23)	f. house, home
dōnec (18)	adv. until
dōnō, āre, āvī, ātum (21)	1, to present, bestow
dormiō, īre, īvī, ītum (19)	4, to sleep
dubitō, āre, āvī, ātum (23)	1, to doubt
dūcō, dūcere, duxī, ductum (5)	3, to lead
dum (8)	adv. while
duo, duae, duo (3)	numerical adj. two
duodecim (14)	indeclinable numeral, twelve
duodecimus, a, um (2)	numerical adj. twelfth
dux, ducis (3)	m. leader

Glossary

ē, ex (1)	prep. + abl. out of, from
Eboracum Oppidum (24)	n. Yorktown
ecclēsia, ae (10)	f. church
edō, edere, ēdī, ēsum (23)	3, to eat, devour
effringō, effringere, effrēgī, effractum (17)	3, to break open
egeō, egēre, eguī (28)	2, (+ gen. or abl.) to need, require
ego (12)	pronoun, I
eheu (6)	interjection (expressing pain) alas!, oh!
emō, emere, ēmī, emptum (11)	3, to buy
emptiō, emptiōnis (28)	f. purchase
eō, īre, īvī, ītum (12)	irregular, to go
equitatio, equitationis (19)	f. horseride
equitō, āre, āvī, ātum (14)	1, to ride (a horse)
equus, ī (14)	m. horse
et (2)	conj. and
etiam (7)	adv. also, even
etiamnunc (4)	adv. even now, at the present time
Europaeī, ōrum (7)	m. Europeans
eventus, ūs (25)	m. outcome
excitō, āre, āvī, ātum (19)	1, to arouse, awaken
excommunicō, āre, āvī, ātum (11)	1, to excommunicate
exemplum, ī (10)	n. example
exercitus, -ūs (4)	m. army
expellō, expellere, expulī, expulsum (28)	3, to expel
explōrātor, explōrātōris (4)	m. explorer
explōrō, āre, āvī, ātum (4)	1, to explore
exsistō, exsistāre, exstitī, exstitum (31)	2, (+dat.) to proceed, arise, issue from
extrā (20)	prep. + acc. outside of

Glossary

Fabianus, a, um (23)	adj. of/pertaining to Fabius Maximus, Roman General and Dictator
fabulōsus, a, um (4)	adj. fabled, famous in stories
faciēs, faciēī (17)	f. face
facilis, facile (7)	adj. easy
faciō, facere, fēcī, factum (3)	3, to do, make, act
factiō, factiōnis (32)	f. party, faction; partisanship
factum, ī (1)	n. deed, act
famēs, famis (7)	f. starvation, famine
familia, ae (4)	f. family
farīna, ae (15)	f. flour
fātum, ī (19)	n. fate
fēcundus, a, um (4)	adj. fertile
fēmina, -ae (7)	f. woman
fenestra, ae (19)	f. window
Ferdinandus, ī (2)	m. Ferdinand
ferō, ferre, tulī, lātum (7)	irregular, to bring, carry
ferox, ferōcis (4)	adj. fierce
ferus, ī (13)	m. wild animal
festīnō, āre, āvī, ātum (14)	1, to hurry
fidēlitās, fidēlitātis (18)	f. loyalty, fidelity
fīlia, ae (6)	f. daughter
fīlius, ī (19)	m. son
fiō, fierī, factus sum (5)	irregular, to become
fiscus, ī (26)	m. finance
flō, āre, āvī, ātum (14)	1, to flow
Flōridus, a, um (4)	adj. flowering, blooming, beautiful
flūmen, flūminis (5)	n. river
fodiō, fodere, fōdī, fossum (24)	3, to dig
foederātus, a, um (25)	adj. united
fons, fontis (4)	m. spring, fountain

Glossary

fōrma, ae (12)	f. form, shape; beauty
fortis, forte (8)	adj. strong, brave
fortūna, ae (7)	f. fortune
Franciscus, ī (31)	m. Francis
fraudō, āre, āvī, ātum (24)	1, to cheat
fretum, ī (3)	n. strait, sound
frīgidus, a, um (23)	adj. cold
frūmentum, ī (9)	n. crop, grain
fugiō, fugere, fūgī, fugitum (5)	3, to flee, escape
fūnambulus, ī (13)	m. tight rope walker
fundo, āre, āvī, ātum (1)	1, to found, build
fundus, ī (13)	m. farm
Gallī, ōrum (5)	m. pl. Frenchmen, the French (people)
Gallia, ae (5)	f. France
gaudeō, gaudēre, gāvīsus sum (20)	2, to rejoice at
gens, gentis (5)	m. tribe, clan; people, nation
geōgraphia, ae (22)	f. geography
Germānia, ae (21)	f. Germany
Germānicus, a, um (21)	adj. German
gerō, gerere, gessī, gestum (19)	3, to wage, carry on; wear
Gorgius, ī (14)	m. George
Graecus, a, um (10)	adj. Greek
grātia, ae (9)	f. grace; gratitude, thanks
gravis, grave (6)	adj. heavy, serious, grave
graviter (24)	adv. heavily
gubernātor, gubernātōris (2)	m. navigator
habeō, habēre, habuī, habitum (11)	2, to have, hold
habitō, āre, āvī, ātum (4)	1, to live, dwell
Henricus, ī (1)	m. Henry
herba, ae (7)	f. grass, plant

Glossary

heri (14)	adv. yesterday
Hibernia, ae (15)	f. Ireland
hībernus, a, um (23)	adj. winter
hic, haec, hoc (1)	demonstrative pronoun/adj. this, these
hiems, hiemis (22)	f. winter
Hispānia, ae (2)	f. Spain
Hispānus, a, um (4)	adj. Spanish
Hispānus, ī (2)	m. Spaniard
hodiē (3)	adv. today
Hondiria, ae (4)	f. Honduras
honestissimus, a, um (26)	adj. most honored
honōrō, āre, āvī, ātum (5)	1, to honor, respect
hōra, ae (8)	f. hour
hortus, ī (13)	m. garden
hostis, hostis (5)	m/f. enemy
iaceō, iacēre, iacuī, iacitum (24)	2, to lie down, lie dead
iaciō, iacere, iēcī, iactum (16)	3, to throw, hurl
Iacobus, ī (7)	m. James
iaculor, iaculārī, iāculatus sum (20)	deponent, to shoot at
iam (7)	adv. now, already
ibi (4)	adv. there
ictus, ūs (24)	m. blow
iēiūnus, a, um (23)	adj. hungry
igitur (21)	adv. therefore
ignis, ignis (7)	m. fire
ille, illa, illud (4)	demonstrative pronoun/adj. that, those
illic (11)	adv. there
immensus, a, um (29)	adj. immense, immeasurable, boundless

Glossary

impellō, impellere, impulī, impulsum (22)	3, to force
impendeō, impendēre, impenduī (32)	2, to threaten, hang over
imperātor, imperātōris (16)	m. general
imperium, ī (4)	n. empire
impetus, ūs (20)	m. attack, advance
in (1)	prep. + acc. into; + abl. in, on
incidō, incidere, incidī, incāsum (7)	3, to happen, occur (with in + acc. - fall upon)
incipiō, incipere, incēpī, inceptum (20)	3, to begin, start
incitō, āre, āvī, ātum (16)	1, to urge on, arouse, incite
incognitus, a, um (29)	adj. unknown
incola, ae (19)	f. settler, colonist
incommodum, ī (7)	n. misfortune
incūriōsus, a, um (32)	adj. regardless, unconcerned, indifferent
India, ae (2)	f. India
indicō, āre, āvī, ātum (2)	1, to indicate
Indigenae, ārum (7)	m. pl. Natives
Indigenus, a, um (5)	adj. native
infans, infantis (12)	m/f. small child, infant
infēlix, infēlīcis (5)	adj. unlucky
infirmus, a, um (7)	adj. weak
ingens, ingentis (4)	adj. huge
iniūria, ae (12)	f. harm, injury; grievance, offense
inscientia, ae (9)	f. lack of knowledge, ignorance
insequens, insequentis (7)	adj. following
insula, ae (3)	f. island
inter (2)	prep. + acc. between
interdum (15)	adv. sometimes

Glossary

interim (11)	adv. meanwhile
interior, interius (11)	comparative adj. interior
intolerābilis, e (18)	adj. intolerable
intrō (26)	prep. + acc. inside
intrō, āre, āvī, ātum (15)	1, to enter
inveniō, invenīre, invēnī, inventum (3)	4, to come upon, find
Iohannes, Iohannis (6)	m. John
Iospehus, ī (19)	m. Joseph
ipse, ipsa, ipsum (23)	intensive adj. himself
īrātus, a, um (18)	adj. angry
is, ea, id (2)	pronoun, he, she, it
Isabella, ae (2)	f. Isabella
iste, ista, istud (16)	demonstrative pronoun/adj., that (of yours)
ita (18)	adv., thus
iter, itineris (6)	n. journey
iterum (2)	adv. again
iubeō, iubēre, iussī, iussum (3)	2, to order
iūdex, iūdicis (26)	m. judge
iūdicium, ī (26)	n. court
Iūlius, ī (21)	m. July
Iūnius, ī (20)	m. June
iūrō, āre, āvī, ātum (27)	1, to swear
iūs, iūris (10)	n. law; (pl.) rights
iuvenis, iuvenis (21)	m/f. young man/woman
iuxtā (7)	prep. + acc., next to, near
labor, labōris (9)	f. work
labōrō, āre, āvī, ātum (9)	1, to work
lacus, lacūs (5)	m. lake
laetus, a, um (27)	adj. happy
lanterna, ae (17)	f. lantern

Glossary

Latīnus, a, um (10)	adj. Latin
laudō, āre, āvī, ātum (20)	1, to praise
Laurentia, ae (5)	m. Lawrence
lectus, ī (19)	m. bed
lēgātus, ī (25)	m. deputy, representative
legō, legere, lēgī, lectum (13)	3, to read; to choose
lex, lēgis (10)	f. law; (pl.) body of laws, constitution
libellus, ī (21)	m. little book
libenter (9)	adv. willingly, gladly
liber, librī (13)	m. book
līberī, līberōrum (12)	m.pl. children
līberō, āre, āvī, ātum (20)	1, to free
lībertās, lībertātis (11)	f., freedom
lībertus, ī (20)	m. freedman
lībra, ae (32)	f. balance, scales
lignum, ī (15)	n. timber, wood
līnea, ae (2)	f. line
lingua, ae (3)	f. tongue, language
līnum, ī (15)	n. flax
littera, ae (10)	f. letter (of alphabet); (pl.) literature
lītus, litoris (5)	n. shore, coast
locus, ī (5)	m. place
longus, a, um (6)	adj. long
Louisiana, ae (28)	f. Louisiana
lūdō, lūdere, lūsī, lūsum (13)	3, to play
Ludovicus, ī (2)	m. Louis
lūdus, ī (1)	m. school; game
lūgeō, lūgēre, luxī (20)	2, to mourn, grieve
Lusitanī, ōrum (1)	m. pl. Portuguese people
Lusitania, ae (1)	f. Portugal
lutum, ī (23)	n. mud

Glossary

lux, lūcis (11)	f. light
Magellanus, ī (3)	m. Magellan
magister, magistrī (1)	m. teacher, captain (of merchant ship)
magistrātus, ūs (21)	m. official
magnus, a, um (2)	adj. big, large
maior, maioris (32)	comparative adj. greater, bigger
male (11)	adv. badly, wrongly
mandātum, ī (29)	n. an order, instruction, commission
mandō, āre, āvī, ātum (2)	1, to entrust
maneō, manēre, mansī, mansum (8)	2, to remain, stay
manus, ūs (17)	f. hand; band (of troops)
mare, maris (3)	n. sea
Massachusettēnsis, e (9)	adj. of Massachusettes
Massaciusetta, ae (2)	f. Massachusettes
māter, mātris (13)	f. mother
mātrimōnium, ī (7)	n. marriage
maximus, a, um (9)	adj. great
mēcum (20)	= cum mē
medicus, ī (19)	m. doctor
medius, a, um (4)	adj. middle
mens, mentis (28)	f. mind
mensis, mensis (2)	m. month
mercātūra, ae (5)	f. trade
merīdiānus, a, um (4)	adj. southern, southernly; midday
messis, messis (9)	f. harvest
mētātor, mētātōris (22)	m. surveyor
meus, a, um (20)	adj. my
migrō, āre, āvī, ātum (4)	1, to move, migrate
mīles, mīlitis (16)	m. soldier, infantryman
mīlitaris, e (23)	adj. military

Glossary

mīlitia, ae (31)	f. military service, the military
mille, milia (8)	n. thousand(s)
minime (2)	adv. no
mīrus, a, um (2)	adj. amazing, wonderful
Mississippiēnsis, e (28)	adj. of the Mississippi
Missuria, ae (32)	f. Missouri
mittō, mittere, mīsī, missum (1)	3, to send, dispatch
modo (7)	adv. only
mōmentum, ī (19)	n. moment
moneō, monēre, monuī, monitum (16)	2, to warn
Montezuma, ae (4)	m. Montezuma, king of Aztecs
morbus, ī (9)	m. sickness, illness
mors, mortis (20)	f. death
mortuus, a, um (9)	adj. dead
mōs, mōris (5)	m. custom
moveō, movēre, mōvī, mōtum (11)	2, to move
mox (7)	adv. soon
mulgeō, mulgēre, mulsī, mulsum (13)	2, to milk
multus, a, um (1)	adj. many
mundō, āre, āvī, ātum (17)	1, to clean
mundus, ī (21)	m. world, mankind
mutō, āre, āvī, ātum (7)	1, to change
mūtuus, a, um (26)	adj. borrowed
nam (5)	adv. for
Napoleon, Napoleonis (27)	m. Napolean Bonaparte
narrātiō, nārratiōnis (29)	f. an account, telling
nārrō, āre, āvī, ātum (12)	1, to tell
nascor, nascī, nātus sum (1)	deponent, to be born
nauta, ae (1)	m. sailor, navigator

Glossary

nautica, ōrum (1)	n. pl. nautical things
nauticus, a, um (1)	adj. nautical, naval
nāvālis, e (5)	adj. naval
navarchus, ī (1)	m. ship's captain
nāvigātiō, nāvigātiōnis (1)	m. voyage, navigation
nāvigō, āre, āvī, ātum (1)	1, to sail
nāvis, nāvis (2)	f. ship
nebula, ae (14)	f. fog, mist
necō, āre, āvī, ātum (3)	1, to kill, execute
negō, āre, āvī, ātum (26)	1, to deny, refuse
nēmō, nēminis (6)	m./f. no one, nobobdy
neptis, neptis (6)	f. granddaughter
neque (16)	adv. (cf. nec) - neither, nor
niger, nigra, nigrum (12)	adj. black
nihil (17)	adv. nothing
nix, nivis (23)	f. snow
nōbilis, e (8)	adj. famous, notable, noble
noceō, nocēre, nocuī, nocitum (12)	2, (+dat.) to harm
nolo, nolle, nolui (20)	irregular, to not wish, want
nōmen, nōminis (5)	n. name
nōn (1)	adv. not
nōnne (24)	interrogative adv. is it not? (non + ne)
nōnus, a, um (8)	numerical adj. ninth
nōs (17)	pronoun, we
noster, nostra, nostrum (20)	adj. our
Nova Anglia (15)	f. New England
Nova Aurelia (28)	f. New Orleans
November, Novembris (8)	m. November (month)
Novum Eboracum (15)	n. New York
novus, nova, novum (2)	adj. new, strange
nox, noctis (12)	f. night

Glossary

nūbēs, nūbis (14)	f. cloud
nūdus, a, um (23)	adj. naked, bare
nullus, a, um (1)	adj. not any, none
numerus, ī (32)	m. number
numquam (1)	adv. never
nunc (5)	adv. now
nūntiō, āre, āvī, ātum (2)	1, to announce
nūntius, ī (14)	m. messenger
ob viam or obviam (24)	adv. (+ dative) to meet
obscūrus, a, um (19)	adj. dark
obsignō, āre, āvī, ātum (26)	1, to sign
obstō, obstāre, obstiti, obstaturus (31)	2, to stand before; hinder, prevent
obtineō, obtinēre, obtinuī, obtentum (21)	2, to take hold of, possess
Occidentalēs Indiae (15)	f. West Indies
occidentalis, e (28)	adj. west
occupātus, a, um (23)	adj. busy
oceanus, ī (2)	m. ocean
Octōber, Octōbris (2)	m. October
octōdecim (21)	indeclinable numeral, eighteen
oculus, ī (20)	m. eye
ōdium, ī (32)	n. hatred, dislike
officium, ī (12)	n. duty, service
omnis, omne (10)	adj. all, every
onus, oneris (8)	n. load, burden; cargo
oppidum, ī (7)	n. town
oppugnō, āre, āvī, ātum (5)	1, to attack
optime (27)	adv. best
optō, āre, āvī, ātum (8)	1, to choose, desire
orbis, orbis (2)	m. circle, globe, world
ostium, ī (28)	n. mouth (of a river)

Glossary

pācificus, a, um (3)	adj. peaceable, peaceful
paeninsula, ae (4)	f. peninsula
parātus, a, um (16)	adj. prepared, ready
parens, parentis (13)	m/f. parent
parō, āre, āvī, ātum (14)	1, to prepare, get ready
pars, partis (20)	f. part
parvus, a, um (20)	adj. small, little
pastor, pastōris (11)	m. shepherd; pastor
pasuus, ūs (8)	m. step, pace; footstep
patefaciō, patefacere, patefēcī, patefactum (1)	3, to make open, make clear
pater, patris (5)	m. father
patibulum, ī (24)	n. gallows
patria, ae (8)	f. fatherland, country
patruus, ī (5)	m. paternal uncle
paucī, ae, a (13)	pl. adj. few
Paulus, ī (19)	m. Paul
pax, pācis (7)	f. peace
pecūnia, ae (1)	f. money
pellis, pellis (8)	f. hide, skin; fur
per (8)	prep. + acc. through, during
perdō, perdere, perdidī, perditum (4)	3, to destroy, ruin
pereō, perīre, perīvī, peritum (9)	irregular, to perish, die
perficiō, perficere, perfēcī, perfactum (3)	3, to complete, finish
perīculum, ī (9)	n. danger
permētior, permētīrī, permensus sum (22)	deponent, to survey
perpetuus, a, um (4)	adj. continuous, eternal
pēs, pedis (23)	m. foot
petō, petere, petīvī, petītum (6)	3, to look for, go in search of

Glossary

Petrus, ī (20)	m. Peter
Philadelphia, ae (15)	f. Philadelphia
Philippinus, a, um (3)	adj. Philippine
pingō, pingere, pinxī, pictum (17)	3, to paint
pila, ae (13)	f. ball
piscis, piscis (15)	m. fish
plānitiēs, ēī (22)	f. plain, level field
plaudō, plaudere, plausī, plausum (27)	3, (+dat.) to applaud
plēnus, a, um (16)	adj. full
plūs (17)	adv. more
plūsquam (1)	adv. more than
Plymuta, ae (8)	f. Plymouth
podium, ī (27)	n. balcony
Polybius, ī (25)	m. Polybius, Greek Historian
pōnō, pōnere, posuī, positum (17)	3, to put, place
pontifex, pontificus (2)	m. priest, pope
populus, ī (14)	m. people
porcus, ī (12)	m. hog, pig
portō, āre, āvī, ātum (1)	1, to carry
possum, posse, posuī (15)	irregular, can, be able
post (4)	prep. + acc. after; adv. after
posteā (11)	adv. afterwards
postrīdiē (20)	adv. the next day, following day
potentia, ae (18)	f. power
potius (23)	adv. rather, instead
praceptum, ī (10)	n. teaching, precept
praedicō, āre, āvī, ātum (14)	1, to preach
praedium, ī (22)	n. estate
praefectus, ī (2)	m. supervisor, commander (+ gen. = supervisor of)
praemium, ī (2)	n. reward

Glossary

praesens, praesentis (6)	adj. present
praesentia, ae (14)	f. presence
praesidens, praesidentis (25)	m. president
praeter (17)	prep. + acc. except
prīmus, a, um (1)	adj. first
prīnceps, prīncipis (1)	m/f. ruler, prince
principiō (22)	adv. at the beginning, at first
prior, prius (31)	comparative adj. prior, former, earlier
prō (2)	prep. + abl. on behalf of, for
probō, āre, āvī, ātum (2)	1, to test, prove
prōcēdō, prōcēdere, processī, processum (16)	3, to proceed, advance
procul (14)	adv. from a distance, far off
proelium, ī (16)	n. battle
propiorus, a, um (24)	adj. (+ dative) nearer to, closer to
prōpositiō, prōpositiōnis, (32)	f. proposition
propter (9)	prep. + acc. on account of, because
prosperus, a, um (26)	adj. successful
prōvoco, āre, āvī, ātum (11)	1, to provoke
prūdentia, ae (21)	f. sense, wisdom
publicus, a, um (25)	adj. of the people, public
puella, ae (13)	f. girl
puer, puerī (7)	m. boy
pugna, ae (5)	f. battle, fight
pugnō, āre, āvī, ātum (16)	1, to fight
pulvis, pulveris (14)	m. dust
pūniō, īre, īvī, ītum (16)	4, to punish, avenge
pūpa, ae (13)	f. doll, puppet
purgō, āre, āvī, ātum (10)	1, to purify, cleanse
Puritanus, ī (10)	m. Puritans
putō, āre, āvī, ātum (2)	1, to think

Glossary

quadrāgintā (7)	numerical adj. forty
quaerō, quaerere, quaesīvī, quaesītum (4)	3, to seek, look for
quālis, quale (12)	interrogative adj. what kind of
quamquam (4)	adv. although
quartus, a, um (21)	numerical adj. fourth
quasi (17)	adv. as if
quattuor (7)	numerical adj. four
quīdam, quaedam, quiddam (3)	adj./pronoun, certain one(s)
quinquāginta (1)	numerical adj. fifty
quinque (3)	indeclinable numerical adj. five
quis, quid (12)	interrogative pronoun, who, what
quod (2)	conj. because
quōmodo (12)	interrogative adv. how, in what way
quondam (29)	adv. once, formerly
quotannīs (15)	adv. yearly
rebelliō, rebelliōnis (26)	f. rebellion, revolution
recēdō, recēdere, recessī, recessum (16)	3, to retreat
receptus, ūs (23)	m. retreat (military)
redeō, redīre, rediī, redītum (2)	irreg., to return, go back
referō, referre, rettulī, relātum (2)	irreg., to bring back
rēgīna, ae (2)	f. queen
regiō, regiōnis (32)	f. territory, region
regō, regere, rexī, rectum (25)	3, to govern, rule
religiō, religiōnis (11)	f. religion
relinquō, relinquere, relīquī, relictum (3)	3, to leave behined, abandon
remaneō, remanēre, remansī (32)	2, to remain, continue
remōtus, a, um (13)	adj. far off, distant
repellō, repellere, reppulī, repulsum (20)	3, to drive back, repel

Glossary

repōnō, repōnere, reposuī, repositum (4)	3, to replace
rēs, rēī (23)	f. thing, matter
respectus, ūs (23)	m. respect
respondeō, respondēre, respondī, responsum (2)	2, to reply, answer to
responsum, ī (18)	n. response
revertō, revertere, revertī, reversus sum (8)	3, to turn back, return
rēx, rēgis (2)	m. king (pl. - monarchs)
rīma, ae (8)	f. crack
rītus, ūs (25)	m. manner, ritual
Rogerus, ī (11)	m. Roger
rogō, āre, āvī, ātum (2)	1, to sail
Rōmānus, a, um (25)	adj. Roman
ruber, rubra, rubrum (11)	adj. red
saeculus, ī (4)	n. generation, century
saepe (8)	adv. often
saevus, a, um (16)	adj. fierce, savage
sagitta, ae (16)	f. arrow
salārium, ī (26)	n. salt; pay
saliō, īre, īvī, ītum (19)	4, to leap, jump
Samuhel (5)	m. Samuel
sanctus, a, um (5)	adj. holy; saint
schola, ae (10)	f. upper school, school of rhetoric; followers
sciō, īre, īvī, ītum (6)	4, to know
scrībō, scrībere, scripsī, scriptum (13)	3, to write
scriptūrae, arum (10)	f.pl. the scriptures
secundus, a, um (26)	adj. second
secūris, secūris (17)	f. hatchet

Glossary

sed (1)	conj. but
sēditiō, sēditiōnis (3)	f. mutiny, armed uprising
sēmen, sēminis (15)	m. seed
sēmisomnis, e (22)	adj. half-asleep
semper (2)	adv. always
sēnātus, ūs (25)	m. senate
sentiō, sentīre, sensī, sensum (16)	4, to sense, feel, perceive
September, Septembri (8)	m. September (month)
septentriōnālis, e (19)	adj. north, northern
sermō, sermōnis (11)	m. conversation, speech, sermon
serō (14)	adv. late
serō, serere, sēvī, satum (9)	2, to sow, plant
serviō, īre, iī, ītum (12)	4, (+dat.) to serve, be a slave to
servitūs, servitūtis (32)	f. slavery
servō, āre, āvī, ātum (26)	1, to save
servus, ī (1)	m. slave
sextus, a, um (8)	numerical adj. sixth
sī (12)	conj. if
sīc (4)	adv. thus
significātiō, significātiōnis (26)	f. significance
signum, ī (17)	n. sign, signal
silentium, ī (17)	n. silence
silva, ae (16)	f. wood, forest
simul (15)	adv. together, at the same time
sine (17)	prep. + abl. without
sitiō, īre, īvī (14)	4, to thirst for
societās, societātis (25)	f. confederation, alliance
socius, ī (6)	m. ally, comrade, friend
sōlitūdinō, sōlitūdinis (21)	f. solitude, loneliness
sollicitus, a, um (18)	adj. worried
sōlus, a, um (8)	adj. only, alone
somnus, ī (19)	m. sleep

Glossary

sonus, ī (17)	m. sound
spādix, spādīcis (19)	adj. chestnut-brown
spectāculum, ī (13)	n. show, entertainment
spectō, āre, āvī, ātum (13)	1, to look at, watch
spectrum, ī (12)	n. apparition
spēs, speī (22)	f. hope
statim (14)	adv. immediately
studeō, studēre, studuī (6)	2, to desire, be eager, be eager for
stupeō, stupēre, stupuī (20)	2, to be stunned, amazed, stupefied
suādeō, suādēre, suāsī, suāsum (2)	2, to urge
subitō (14)	adv. immediately
subsidium, ī (21)	n. military support
succēdō, succēdere, sucessī, sucessum (31)	3, to come up under; (mil.) to march on, advance, approach
suffrāgātōr, suffrāgātōris (27)	m. voter, elector
sum, esse, fuī, futūrum (1)	irreg. to be
summus, a, um (22)	adj. highest
superbia, ae (16)	f. pride
superstes, superstitis (3)	m. noun or adj. survivor
suprā (14)	prep. + acc. above; adv. above
suprēmus, a, um (26)	adj. highest, supreme
sursum (5)	adv. up
sustineō, sustinēre, sustinuī, sustentum (32)	3, to uphold, support
suus, a, um (11)	adj. his/her/its own
taberna, ae (17)	f. tavern, shop, inn
tamen (4)	adv. nevertheless
tandem (2)	adv. finally
tardus, a, um (28)	adj. slow
telum, ī (22)	n. weapon
tempus, temporis (7)	n. time
teneō, tenēre, tenuī, tentum (19)	2, to hold

Glossary

tentōrium, ī (23)	n. tent
terminō, āre, āvī, ātum (18)	1, to limit
terra, ae (2)	f. earth, world
terreō, terrēre, terruī, territum (21)	2, to scare, frighten
tertius, a, um (20)	numerical adj. third
thea, ae (17)	f. tea
Thoma, ae (10)	m. Thomas
tignum, ī (23)	n. log, trunk
timeō, timēre, timuī (12)	2, to be afraid, fear
tintinnābulum, ī (19)	n. bell
Tisquantus, ī (9)	m. Squanto
toga, ae (19)	f. toga, garment
tollō, tollere, sustulī, sublātum (18)	3, to lift, raise
tormentum, ī (16)	n. artillery piece, gun; n.pl. artillery
tōtus, a, um (6)	adj. whole, all
tractō, āre, āvī, ātum (19)	1, to pull
trāditiō, trāditiōnis (11)	f. tradition
trādō, trādere, trādidī, trādidtum (24)	3, to hand over, surrender
trādūcō, trādūcere, trāduxī, trāductum (11)	3, to disgrace, dishonor
trahō, trahere, traxī, tractum (12)	3, to drag, pull
trāns (6)	prep. + acc. across
trānseō, trānsīre, trānsīvī, trānsitum (22)	irreg. to go across, cross
trecentī, ae, a (7)	numerical adj. three hundred
trēs, tria, trēs (2)	numerical adj. three
tū (12)	pronoun, you
tugurium, ī (23)	n. cabin
turba, ae (27)	f. crowd

Glossary

tuus, tua, tuum (12)	adj. your
tympanum, ī (24)	n. drum
ubī (5)	adv. when; interrog. adv. where?
ubīque (6)	adv. everywhere
ūnus, a, um (1)	adj. one
ūsus, ūs (22)	m. skill, art
uterque, utraque, utrumque (32)	adj. each (of the two)
ūtor, ūtī, ūsus sum (28)	deponent (+abl.), to use
uxor, uxōris (14)	f. wife
vacca, ae (13)	f. cow
vallis, vallis (23)	f. valley
vallum, ī (24)	n. rampart, trench
varius, a, um (32)	adj. various
Vasingtonia, ae (31)	f. Washington D.C.
Vasingtonius, ī (16)	m. Washington
vector, vectōris (8)	m. passenger (on a ship)
vendō, vendere, vendidī, venditum (28)	3, to sell
veniō, venīre, vēnī, vēntum (1)	4, to come
verberō, āre, āvī, ātum (26)	1, to beat
verbum, ī (17)	n. word
vērus, a, um (1)	adj. true
vestis, vestis (13)	f. clothing
vetus, veteris (4)	adj. old, ancient
via, ae (1)	f. road, way, street
vīcīnus, a, um (22)	adj. nearby, neighboring
victōria, ae (4)	f. victory
videō, vidēre, vīdī, vīsum (2)	2, to see
vīgintī (8)	indecl. numeral twenty
vincō, vincere, vīcī, victum (4)	3, to conquer, win
vinculum, ī (26)	n. chain; n.pl. prison
vīnum, ī (8)	n. wine

Glossary

vir, virī (7)	m. man, husband
Virginia, ae (21)	f. Virginia
viridis, viride (7)	adj. green
virtūs, virtūtis (20)	f. bravery
vīsitō, āre, āvī, ātum (20)	1, to visit
vītō, āre, āvī, ātum (18)	1, to avoid
vīvō, vīvere, vixī, victum (7)	3, to live, be alive
volō, velle, voluī (7)	irreg. to wish, want
vulgāris, e (21)	adj. common
vulnerō, āre, āvī, ātum (16)	1, to wound

About the Author

Karen Moore began her study of Latin in seventh grade, and added Greek to her linguistic studies during her college years. In 1994, she was awarded the Ruth and Myron G. Kuhlman Scholarship in Classics. Karen graduated from the University of Texas at Austin in 1996 with a Bachelor of Arts in Classics and a minor in History. Since that time she has taught Latin to students in grades three through twelve through a wide variety of venues, including home-school, public school, and Classical Christian schools. She is currently serving as the chair of the Latin Department at Grace Academy of Georgetown, a Classical Christian school located in the heart of Texas. She is a member of the American Classical League, the Texas Classical Association, and serves as the sponsor of Grace Academy's Latin Club.

Karen and her husband, Bryan, have three children who attend school at Grace Academy.

About the Editor

Gaylan DuBose graduated with high honors from the University of North Texas in 1964 and received his Master of Arts in Classics from the University of Minnesota in 1970 He has also studied at the University of Texas and at Worcester College, Oxford University, England. He was the academic contest chair for the National Junior Classical League from 1996 through 2005. He currently is teaching at St. Andrew's Episcopal School in Austin, Texas, and is in his forty-third year as a classroom teacher. He is the author of Farrago Latina: A Teacher Resource and co-author of Excelability in Advanced Latin. He is an avid reader and is the organist and minister of music at St. Augustine's Orthodox Catholic Church and Pro-Cathedral in Pflugerville, Texas.

ANSWER KEY

Looking for the answers to this book?
Download and print the answers (PDF)
for <u>free</u> from our website at:

www.classicalacademicpress.com/lfc_history.html

stay tuned!

Classical Latin, Creatively taught
LATIN for children
ACTIVITY BOOK!

Primer C

ROB BADDORF &
DR. CHRISTOPHER PERRIN

With over one hundred pages of games, puzzles and fun, this book makes mastery of the classic language a blast! The activity book accompanies **Latin For Children: Primer C**, following chapter by chapter, to supplement and enhance your practice of Latin vocabulary and grammar.